Hebrew Bible

Book of
Leviticus

Five books of Moses

SimchatChaim.com

There is no known book without mistakes. Therefore, I ask in every language of application if anyone has any questions, comments, clarifications, corrections, please send to: simchatchaim@yahoo.com

All material used in this section may not be used for commercial purposes, but only for study and teaching.

To get this book or books and information Email me at:

simchatchaim@yahoo.com

מהדורה שניה תשפ"ד
Second edition 2024

The contents of the book

Page   **Chapter**

Introduction to the

Jewish Bible

First you need to know that the Bible was originally written in the holy language, which today is called Hebrew.

The Tanach itself went through a series of translations from language to language until today's English language.

As a whole, the Tanakh was translated from the holy language into Greek, and from Greek into Latin, and from there into the ancient Agalic, and then into the more modern English.

The problem is when translating from language to language the original meaning is lost.

In the translation of languages there is no realistic possibility to make a completely accurate translation, since in every language there are several translation options for most words, and each word has a different connotation, and also differs to a certain extent from the exact connotation of the original word in the source language.

For example, it is possible to translate the word - שמים. **sky** into English for Sky and Heaven. Two suitable options that each have a different meaning from the other, and also slightly different from the full connotation of the word **sky** שמים. For this reason, along with the attempt to bridge the cultural difference, every translation is actually also an interpretation. In many cases, the translators took the approach of **extensive translation**, in which the translation adds details and interpretations beyond the original text, changes the content, and describes what is happening in a way that is more suitable to the cultural concepts accepted for the period and region. In the common translations these changes are found - to a certain degree of change - in tens of percent of the verses. The general public in these periods knew the Bible only from the translations, and therefore in different regions they actually knew different versions of the same texts, according to the local halachic belief.

The most classic example of this is this:
In the book of Exodus chapter 34 verse 29 it is explained that - KARAN [קרן] the skin of Moses face.

The word KARAN [קרן] has at least two meanings:
A. Radiant.
B. A horn, like that of a bull.
There are other meanings to this word that do not belong to this introduction.

An incorrect translation of the Book of Exodus by Jerome [the Vulgate] into Latin led to an error in the interpretation of the phrase - The horn of the skin of his face. [Exodus 34:29]. And because of this, in

Renaissance sculptures, Moshe's forehead was added **Horns**.

And this is the verse in its entirety according to our translation [compare it to your Bible] - So Moses came down from Mount Sinai. And as Moses came down from the mountain bearing the two tablets of the Pact, Moses was not aware that the skin of his face was **radiant**, since he had spoken with God.

It is known that Hebrew has a vowel for every word. And there can be a word that has a different vowel from the same word. For example, the word with four letters - מ.ד.ב.ר

מְדַבֵּר - speaker.

מִדְבָּר - desert.

מַדְבֵּר - A speaking man.

מְדָבָר - out of nothing.

מְדֻבַּר - thing that is being discussed.

There are **only** five vowels with the same word, and really this word has 25 vowel types!!!! which can change the entire meaning of the verse and the translation.

The first translations of the Bible were created by Jews at the beginning of the first millennium AD. During this period, most Jews gradually stopped using the Hebrew language, especially biblical Hebrew. A translated Bible became a basic necessity for the reading of the Torah in the synagogues, which was performed by two people - one who read the verse is in the original language, and an interpreter repeats his words in the spoken language.

The first translations of the Bible were created by Jews at the beginning of the first millennium AD. During this period, most Jews gradually stopped using the Hebrew language, especially biblical Hebrew. A translated Bible became a basic necessity for the reading of the Torah in the synagogues, which was performed by two people - one who read the verse is in the original language, and an interpreter repeats his words in the spoken language.

The Bible translations can be divided into two main types - Jewish translations and Christian translations. There are a number of differences between the two, the most prominent of which is the inclusion of the New Testament in Christian translations as opposed to its absence in Jewish translations. The Jewish translations were made mainly from the original Hebrew text, and most of the early Jewish translations were made only into separate parts of the Bible, with the intention that they will be used as a commentary on the Bible. In contrast, the Christian translations are mostly intended for independent use, and most of them are based on the Greek translation translated into Latin - the Latin Vulgate.

The truth is that the Holy Scriptures should not be translated into any language. But because of an act explained in the Talmud there was no choice and the Jews translated it.

And the story is:
And this was due to the incident of King Ptolemy, as it is taught in a Baraita: There was an incident involving King Ptolemy of Egypt, who assembled seventy-two Elders from the Sages of Israel, and put them into seventy-two separate rooms, and did not reveal to them for what purpose he assembled them, so that they would not coordinate their responses. He entered and approached each and every one, and said to each of them: Write for me a translation of the Torah of Moses your teacher. The Holy One, Blessed be He, placed wisdom in the heart of each and every one, and they all agreed to one common understanding. Not only did they all translate the text correctly, they all introduced the same changes into the translated text.

And the Talmud [Megillah 9a] continues to say that all 72 sages did not translate it exactly, but changed several verses, for example:

And they wrote for him: God created in the beginning [**Bereshit**], reversing the order of the words in the first phrase in the Torah that could be misinterpreted as: **Bereshit created God** [Genesis 1:1]. Instead of: Come, let us go down, and there confound their language [Genesis 11:7], which indicates multiple authorities, they wrote in the singular: Come, let me go down, and there confound their language. In addition, they replaced the verse: "And Sarah laughed within herself [**bekirba**] [Genesis 18:12], with: And Sarah laughed among her relatives [**bikroveha**].

They made this change to distinguish between Sarah's laughter, which God criticized, and Abraham's laughter, to which no reaction is recorded. Based on the change, Sarah's laughter was offensive because she voiced it to others....

The church father Hieronymus [about 325-420], who knew Hebrew in addition to Latin and Greek, and specialized in theology, created an improved homogenous translation from all the Latin translations. In his work, which was done between the years 390-405, he was greatly assisted by the Jews he knew. The translation of the first books he dealt with [first prophets, Samuel and kings] was done closely to the Hebrew text, but the last books [Joshua, Judges, Ruth and Esther] were translated by him in a freer manner. In any case, Hieronymus relied on the Hebrew version, because he noticed the deviations that the Greek translations have from the Hebrew original.

The Vulgate was recognized by the Church in 1546 as the authoritative text of the Holy Scriptures. It includes, apart from the books of the Bible and the New Testament, also the translation of the external books. The name **Vulgate** [=Common] can be translated by Roger Bacon, and when the internal division into chapters was made in the Vulgate.

The English translation - a translation of parts of the Bible into English was made starting from the 7th century. A complete translation of the Bible into English, made under the direction of John Wycliffe, from the Latin version of the Vulgate, was published in about 1380. The church condemned this translation, because it saw the interpretation that accompanied it as heretical. Further English translations were also rejected by the church and the king.

In 1530 William Tyndale translated only the Pentateuch from the Greek in the Kaspela edition into English, and 5 years later Miles Coverdale published the entire Bible in English. James I, King of England initiated the creation of an official translation of the Bible and the New Testament into English. His initiative came against the background of the bitter struggle between Protestants and Catholics in England and Scotland. King James proposed to write a new English translation that would be acceptable to Protestants and Catholics alike. This translation, made from Hebrew and Greek, was published in 1611, and is called the "King James Version, KJV". This translation is still considered the authorized translation of the English Bible [Authorized Version]; Researchers from the universities of London, Oxford and Cambridge worked on it. They also used a Jewish commentary for the translation. In this edition, King James demanded to cleanse the kings of any evil that could cling to them, in order to purify the institution of the monarchy. In the translation, an effort was made to maintain the structure of the Hebrew text, and to convert as much as possible a Hebrew word into an English word. However, a Hebrew word may be translated into different words in English in different contexts, this is to keep the language fluid. The attempt to literally translate Hebrew idioms created new expressions in English, which gradually became part of the English language and culture.

The book of Leviticus

Sefer Vayikra [Book of Leviticus] is the third book of the five pentacles of the Torah. The name is derived from the first word in which the book opens: And Moses was called, and God spoke to him from the tent of meeting to say. The book Vayikra is also known by its Talmudic nickname **Torat Kohanim** [The laws of the Priests], which it earned because it mainly deals with the laws of sacrificial offerings and other laws of the **Mishkan** [Tabernacle].

As mentioned, the bulk of the book deals with mitzvot, sacrifices and various laws, and it contains only two short sections with a narrative tone [the description of the seven days of reserve and the story of the curser].

According to the Midrash, the book of Vayikra that opens this Pentateuch is the first Parshah that the children of Israel learn, and this is for the reason that - they will come pure [children who have not yet sinned] and engage in purity.

Mitzvot of sacrifices [chapters 1-7]
As a continuation of the book of Exodus, which ends

with the completion of the tabernacle and its construction, the book of Leviticus opens with the details of the sacrificial commandments, and specifies the order of sacrifices of the pilgrim, the offerer, the completers, the guilty party, the guilty party and the guilty party. After that, the Torah commands the Priest to take ashes of the burnt offering, and adds various details to the mitzvah of the offering, sinning, God, thanking, and making amends. In the middle of the Laws of the offering which one can eat, there is also a ban on eating forbidden fat of an animal.

The seven days of the reserve [chapters 8-10]
Moshe, Aaron and his sons fulfill the commandment commanded in the book of Exodus 29:1-17, to offer sacrifices and sanctify with them and the anointing oil of the altar, the tabernacle, the priests and their garments. This mitzvah lasts seven days. On the eighth day Aharon and his sons enter their duties with special sacrifices for that day. Fire comes out from before God and consumes the burnt offering and the forbidden fat on the altar. **Nadav and Abihu**, Aaron's two eldest sons, offer foreign incense. They are punished by death. Aharon and his two remaining sons, Eleazar and Itamar, are ordered not to practice mourning customs on them. Aharon and his sons are commanded to forbid drinking wine before and during work and are appointed to teach the Torah to

the people, with an emphasis on the laws of purity and impurity. Moshe commands Aaron and his sons to eat from the portions of the sacrifices. There is a discussion regarding the scapegoats [pair of kid goats] one was burned and the other one was thrown from the mountain.

Laws of impurity and purity: foods, childbirth, wounds, and blood [chapters 11-15]

In the chapters mentioned above the laws of animals that are kosher to eat and impure are detailed, and the details of the impurity of carrion. Then the laws of the purity of the mother and her sacrifice are detailed. The mitzvot of circumcision is mentioned on the eighth day. At the end of the mentioned chapters, come the laws of leprosy of the body, the garment and the house, and the laws of leprosy and leprosy.

Order of Yom Kippur work [chapter 16]

The chapter opens with the prohibition on Aaron the priest to enter the Holy of Holies at any time. The Torah lists the sacrifices he must bring when he comes - a sacrificial bull, a ram for the burnt offering and two goats - and the order of their sacrifice and the burning of the incense before and after. Two goats were assigned lots, **to God** and **to hell**: the one belonging to God was sacrificed for sin, and the other was sent to carry the sins of Israel to the land of judgment in the desert. The Torah points out the time when this arrangement must be made - once a year, on Yom Kippur - and adds details of laws that practice it, such as torture of the soul and the prohibition of work.

Prohibition of foreign slaughter and blood prohibition [Chapter 17]

In this chapter, the Torah forbids slaughtering animals outside the camp, without throwing the blood on the altar of God in the tent of meeting [and this as a removal from the work of the shepherds that they were used to]. The Torah extends the prohibition of eating blood as well as the mitzvah to cover the blood of animals and birds.

Prohibition of celibacy [chapter 18]

The Torah forbids walking in the laws of the land of Egypt as well as the land of Canaan, and lists the types of celibacy, that is - prohibitions of sexual contact. This includes the nakedness of a father, mother, father's wife, sister, son's daughter, daughter's daughter, father's wife's daughter, father's sister, mother's sister, father's brother, father's brother's wife, son's wife, brother's wife, wife and daughter, son's daughter or daughter's daughter, two sisters, Nida, a man's wife, in the middle comes the prohibition of the – **Molech** [a person who sacrifices his son] which is not a pubic hair but an idolatry. Do not have carnal relations with any beast and defile yourself thereby. Likewise for a woman: she shall not lend herself to a beast to mate with it; it is perversion. The Torah threatens punishment - **and the earth will spew you up.**

Civil and moral laws, and differentiation from the ways of the idols [chapter 19]

After a short opening that requires us to be holy, and details about the sacred time and place, most of this chapter deals with civil consideration [the equivalent of criminal law nowadays, but including moral requirements], and separation from idolatrous leadership. In these sets of laws, the book mentions set of laws that are also found in other pentacles [such as Exodus], and despite the **sacred** image of the book, the commandment **Love your neighbor as yourself** - for example - is taken precisely from this set of laws [Leviticus 19:18]. The chapter opens with a general mitzvah - **Be holy** and immediately after it deals with the sanctified time and place: keeping the Sabbath. Prohibition of turning to idols, and limiting the time of eating sacrifices [prohibition of remaining and breaking]. The main part of the chapter deals with the commandment of civil consideration. Consideration of the poor and the old. The precepts of civil law: prohibition of theft, denial, lying, false swearing, adultery, robbery, withholding of wages. Consideration of the weak: prohibition of cursing a deaf person, misleading a blind person, and biasing a judge. Responsibility and civil brotherhood: the prohibition of gossiping, the prohibition of avoiding salvation and the prohibition of hatred in the heart. The mitzvot of rebuke, and the prohibition of cleaning and leaving. The mitzvah of separation: animal hybrids, seed hybrids, Shatanz [mixing of wool with linen] and the mitzvah female slave [combination of a free man and a female slave]. The proper behavior in Israel [and differences from the ways of the idolaters]: prohibition of foreskin, prohibition of eating blood, divination, circling the wig and mutilation of the beard, scratching a dead person and writing a tattoo, fornicating with your daughter, the commandment of keeping Shabbat [compared to the idolaters] and fear of the temple, prohibition of **Ob** [idolatry] And God, the compilation of an old man and return [probably in contrast to idolaters], the prohibition of defrauding a resident [in contrast to the behavior of the Egyptians], and the commandment of the truth of measurements and weights.

Chastity penalties [chapter 20]
In this chapter, a specific punishment is detailed for the one who transfers his son and daughter to **Molech** and for all types of celibacy mentioned in chapter 18.

The holiness of the priests, and some sacred laws [chapters 21-22]

In this chapter the priests are warned against defilement with the impurity of a dead person. Ordinary priests [the **laymen**] are allowed to defile their relatives, **a high priest** - cannot. The priests are also warned against marrying a prostitute, convert or a divorcee, and the high priest - is also forbidden to marry a widow. Priests with disabilities are also prohibited from offering sacrifices. Impure priests, or foreign people [who are not priests], are prohibited from eating offerings and consecrations. The laws of the resident priest and his tenant, servant, sons and daughters are also explained. It is also forbidden to bring sacrifices from animals with disabilities. It is forbidden to sacrifice due to lack of time. It is forbidden to slaughter an animal and its son in one day. The Torah repeats the prohibition of remaining. These chapters end with the prohibition of blasphemy and the commandment to sanctify God.

Mitzvot of the holidays [chapter 23]
This chapter deals with the dates of the year. Shabbat, the Passover sacrifice, the holiday of unleavened bread, the Omer offering, the counting of the Omer, Shavuot, Rosh Hashanah, Yom Kippur, Sukkot and Shemini Atzerat are mentioned.

The perpetual candle, the face bread and the blasphemy [chapter 24]
In this chapter, the Torah repeats the Parashat **Ner**

HaTamid [candle that was always light in the temple], details the laws of bread and tells the story of the blasphemer and his punishment. Following the act of blasphemy, additional penalties are imposed on those who blaspheme, hit a person, hit an animal, and mutilate a person.

Shemita, Jubilee and related laws [chapter 25-26]

In this chapter are detailed the laws of shemita, the tributary, the redemption of the land, the prohibition of usury, the laws of a Hebrew slave, the redemption of a slave sold to a Gentile, the prohibition of a statue, a gravestone, and a stone.

The Rebuke [Chapter 26]

In this chapter there are blessings if the Israelites keeping the Torah, and curses if they do not obey it. At the end of the curses came a promise - And I remembered my covenant... and even this, being in the land of their enemies, I will not be afraid...

Commandments of Values and Prohibitions [Chapter 27]

In this chapter come the laws of the desecration of human values, the laws of consecrating a **pure** or **unclean** [defective] animal, the consecration of a house, a manor field, or a field of inheritance, as well as the laws of the firstborn, the laws of prohibition, the second tithe and its redemption, the tithe of an animal, and the laws of compensation.

Leviticus

Vayikra

Chapter 1

1. And the LORD called unto Moses, and spoke unto him out of the tent of meeting, saying:

2. Speak unto the children of Israel, and say unto them: When any man of you bringeth an offering unto the LORD, ye shall bring your offering of the cattle, even of the herd or of the flock.

3. If his offering be a burnt-offering of the herd, he shall offer it a male without blemish; he shall bring it to the door of the tent of meeting, that he may be accepted before the LORD.

4. And he shall lay his hand upon the head of the burnt-offering; and it shall be accepted for him to make atonement for him.

5. And he shall kill the bullock before the LORD; and Aaron's sons, the priests, shall present the blood, and dash the blood round about against the altar that is at the door of the tent of meeting.

6. And he shall flay the burnt-offering, and cut it into its pieces.

7. And the sons of Aaron the priest shall put fire upon the altar, and lay wood in order upon the fire.

8. And Aaron's sons, the priests, shall lay the pieces, and the head, and the suet, in order upon the wood that is on the fire which is upon the altar;

9. But its inwards and its legs shall he wash with water; and the priest shall make the whole smoke on the altar, for a burnt-offering, an offering made by fire, of a sweet savour unto the LORD.

10. And if his offering be of the flock, whether of the sheep, or of the goats, for a burnt-offering, he shall offer it a male without blemish.

11. And he shall kill it on the side of the altar northward before the LORD; and Aaron's sons, the priests, shall dash its blood against the altar round about.

12. And he shall cut it into its pieces; and the priest shall lay them, with its head and its suet, in order on the wood that is on the fire which is upon the altar.

13. But the inwards and the legs shall he wash with water; and the priest shall offer the whole, and make it smoke upon the altar; it is a burnt-offering, an offering made by fire, of a sweet savour unto the LORD.

14. And if his offering to the LORD be a burnt-offering of fowls, then he shall bring his offering of turtle-doves, or of young pigeons.

15. And the priest shall bring it unto the altar, and pinch off its head, and make it smoke on the altar; and the blood thereof shall be drained out on the side of the altar.

16. And he shall take away its crop with the feathers thereof, and cast it beside the altar on the east part, in the place of the ashes.

17. And he shall rend it by the wings thereof, but shall not divide it asunder; and the priest shall make it smoke upon the altar, upon the wood that is upon the fire; it is a burnt-offering, an offering made by fire, of a sweet savour unto the LORD.

Chapter 2

1. And when any one bringeth a meal-offering unto the LORD, his offering shall be of fine flour; and he shall pour oil upon it, and put frankincense thereon.

2. And he shall bring it to Aaron's sons the priests; and he shall take thereout his handful of the fine flour thereof, and of the oil thereof, together with all the frankincense thereof; and the priest shall make the memorial-part thereof smoke upon the altar, an offering made by fire, of a sweet savour unto the LORD.

3. But that which is left of the meal-offering shall be Aaron's and his sons; it is a thing most holy of the offerings of the LORD made by fire.

4. And when thou bringest a meal-offering baked in the oven, it shall be unleavened cakes of fine flour mingled with oil, or unleavened wafers spread with oil.

5. And if thy offering be a meal-offering baked on a griddle, it shall be of fine flour unleavened, mingled with oil.

6. Thou shalt break it in pieces, and pour oil thereon;

it is a meal-offering.

7. And if thy offering be a meal-offering of the stewing-pan, it shall be made of fine flour with oil.

8. And thou shalt bring the meal-offering that is made of these things unto the LORD; and it shall be presented unto the priest, and he shall bring it unto the altar.

9. And the priest shall take off from the meal-offering the memorial-part thereof, and shall make it smoke upon the altar-an offering made by fire, of a sweet savour unto the LORD.

10. But that which is left of the meal-offering shall be Aaron's and his sons; it is a thing most holy of the offerings of the LORD made by fire.

11. No meal-offering, which ye shall bring unto the LORD, shall be made with leaven; for ye shall make no leaven, nor any honey, smoke as an offering made by fire unto the LORD.

12. As an offering of first-fruits ye may bring them unto the LORD; but they shall not come up for a sweet savour on the altar.

13. And every meal-offering of thine shalt thou season with salt; neither shalt thou suffer the salt of the covenant of thy God to be lacking from thy meal-offering; with all thy offerings thou shalt offer salt.

14. And if thou bring a meal-offering of first-fruits unto the LORD, thou shalt bring for the meal-offering of thy first-fruits corn in the ear parched with fire, even groats of the fresh ear.

15. And thou shalt put oil upon it, and lay frankincense thereon; it is a meal-offering.

16. And the priest shall make the memorial-part of it smoke, even of the groats thereof, and of the oil thereof, with all the frankincense thereof; it is an offering made by fire unto the LORD.

Chapter 3

1. And if his offering be a sacrifice of peace-offerings: if he offer of the herd, whether male or female, he shall offer it without blemish before the LORD.

2. And he shall lay his hand upon the head of his offering, and kill it at the door of the tent of meeting; and Aaron's sons the priests shall dash the blood against the altar round about.

3. And he shall present of the sacrifice of peace-offerings an offering made by fire unto the LORD: the fat that covereth the inwards, and all the fat that is upon the inwards,

4. And the two kidneys, and the fat that is on them, which is by the loins, and the lobe above the liver, which he shall take away hard by the kidneys.

5. And Aaron's sons shall make it smoke on the altar upon the burnt-offering, which is upon the wood that is on the fire; it is an offering made by fire, of a sweet savour unto the LORD.

6. And if his offering for a sacrifice of peace-offerings unto the LORD be of the flock, male or female, he shall offer it without blemish.

7. If he bring a lamb for his offering, then shall he present it before the LORD.

8. And he shall lay his hand upon the head of his offering, and kill it before the tent of meeting; and Aaron's sons shall dash the blood thereof against the altar round about.

9. And he shall present of the sacrifice of peace-offerings an offering made by fire unto the LORD: the fat thereof, the fat tail entire, which he shall take away hard by the rump-bone; and the fat that covereth the inwards, and all the fat that is upon the inwards,

10. And the two kidneys, and the fat that is upon them, which is by the loins, and the lobe above the liver, which he shall take away by the kidneys.

11. And the priest shall make it smoke upon the altar; it is the food of the offering made by fire unto the LORD.

12. And if his offering be a goat, then he shall present it before the LORD.

13. And he shall lay his hand upon the head of it, and kill it before the tent of meeting; and the sons of Aaron shall dash the blood thereof against the altar round about.

14. And he shall present thereof his offering, even an offering made by fire unto the LORD: the fat that covereth the inwards, and all the fat that is upon the inwards,

15. And the two kidneys, and the fat that is upon

them, which is by the loins, and the lobe above the liver, which he shall take away by the kidneys.

16. And the priest shall make them smoke upon the altar; it is the food of the offering made by fire, for a sweet savour; all the fat is the LORD'S.

17. It shall be a perpetual statute throughout your generations in all your dwellings, that ye shall eat neither fat nor blood.

Chapter 4

1. And the LORD spoke unto Moses, saying:

2. Speak unto the children of Israel, saying: If any one shall sin through error, in any of the things which the LORD hath commanded not to be done, and shall do any one of them:

3. If the anointed priest shall sin so as to bring guilt on the people, then let him offer for his sin, which he hath sinned, a young bullock without blemish unto the LORD for a sin-offering.

4. And he shall bring the bullock unto the door of the tent of meeting before the LORD; and he shall lay his hand upon the head of the bullock, and kill the bullock before the LORD.

5. And the anointed priest shall take of the blood of the bullock, and bring it to the tent of meeting.

6. And the priest shall dip his finger in the blood, and sprinkle of the blood seven times before the LORD, in front of the veil of the sanctuary.

7. And the priest shall put of the blood upon the horns

of the altar of sweet incense before the LORD, which is in the tent of meeting; and all the remaining blood of the bullock shall he pour out at the base of the altar of burnt-offering, which is at the door of the tent of meeting.

8. And all the fat of the bullock of the sin-offering he shall take off from it; the fat that covereth the inwards, and all the fat that is upon the inwards,

9. And the two kidneys, and the fat that is upon them, which is by the loins, and the lobe above the liver, which he shall take away by kidneys,

10. As it is taken off from the ox of the sacrifice of peace-offerings; and the priest shall make them smoke upon the altar of burnt-offering.

11. But the skin of the bullock, and all its flesh, with its head, and with its legs, and its inwards, and its dung,

12. Even the whole bullock shall he carry forth without the camp unto a clean place, where the ashes are poured out, and burn it on wood with fire; where the ashes are poured out shall it be burnt.

13. And if the whole congregation of Israel shall err, the thing being hid from the eyes of the assembly, and do any of the things which the LORD hath commanded not to be done, and are guilty:

14. When the sin wherein they have sinned is known, then the assembly shall offer a young bullock for a sin-offering, and bring it before the tent of meeting.

15. And the elders of the congregation shall lay their

hands upon the head of the bullock before the LORD; and the bullock shall be killed before the LORD.

16. And the anointed priest shall bring of the blood of the bullock to the tent of meeting.

17. And the priest shall dip his finger in the blood, and sprinkle it seven times before the LORD, in front of the veil.

18. And he shall put of the blood upon the horns of the altar which is before the LORD, that is in the tent of meeting, and all the remaining blood shall he pour out at the base of the altar of burnt-offering, which is at the door of the tent of meeting.

19. And all the fat thereof shall he take off from it, and make it smoke upon the altar.

20. Thus, shall he do with the bullock; as he did with the bullock of the sin-offering, so shall he do with this; and the priest shall make atonement for them, and they shall be forgiven.

21. And he shall carry forth the bullock without the camp, and burn it as he burned the first bullock; it is the sin-offering for the assembly.

22. When a ruler sinneth, and doeth through error any one of all the things which the LORD his God hath commanded not to be done, and is guilty:

23. If his sin, wherein he hath sinned, be known to him, he shall bring for his offering a goat, a male without blemish.

24. And he shall lay his hand upon the head of the goat, and kill it in the place where they kill the burnt-offering before the LORD; it is a sin-offering.

25. And the priest shall take of the blood of the sin-offering with his finger, and put it upon the horns of the altar of burnt-offering, and the remaining blood thereof shall he pour out at the base of the altar of burnt-offering.

26. And all the fat thereof shall he make smoke upon the altar, as the fat of the sacrifice of peace-offerings; and the priest shall make atonement for him as concerning his sin, and he shall be forgiven.

27. And if any one of the common people sin through error, in doing any of the things which the LORD hath commanded not to be done, and be guilty:

28. If his sin, which he hath sinned, be known to him, then he shall bring for his offering a goat, a female without blemish, for his sin which he hath sinned.

29. And he shall lay his hand upon the head of the sin-offering, and kill the sin-offering in the place of burnt-offering.

30. And the priest shall take of the blood thereof with his finger, and put it upon the horns of the altar of burnt-offering, and all the remaining blood thereof shall he pour out at the base of the altar.

31. And all the fat thereof shall he take away, as the fat is taken away from off the sacrifice of peace-offerings; and the priest shall make it smoke upon the altar for a sweet savour unto the LORD; and the priest shall make atonement for him, and he shall be forgiven.

32. And if he bring a lamb as his offering for a sin-offering, he shall bring it a female without blemish.

33. And he shall lay his hand upon the head of the sin-offering, and kill it for a sin-offering in the place where they kill the burnt-offering.

34. And the priest shall take of the blood of the sin-offering with his finger, and put it upon the horns of the altar of burnt-offering, and all the remaining blood thereof shall he pour out at the base of the altar.

35. And all the fat thereof shall he take away, as the fat of the lamb is taken away from the sacrifice of peace-offerings; and the priest shall make them smoke on the altar, upon the offerings of the LORD made by fire; and the priest shall make atonement for him as touching his sin that he hath sinned, and he shall be forgiven.

Chapter 5

1. And if any one sin, in that he heareth the voice of adjuration, he being a witness, whether he hath seen or known, if he do not utter it, then he shall bear his iniquity;

2. Or if any one touch any unclean thing, whether it be the carcass of an unclean beast, or the carcass of unclean cattle, or the carcass of unclean swarming things, and be guilty, it being hidden from him that he is unclean;

3. Or if he touch the uncleanness of man, whatsoever his uncleanness be wherewith he is unclean, and it be hid from him; and, when he knoweth of it, be guilty;

4. Or if any one swear clearly with his lips to do evil, or to do good, whatsoever it be that a man shall utter clearly with an oath, and it be hid from him; and, when he knoweth of it, be guilty in one of these things;

5. And it shall be, when he shall be guilty in one of these things, that he shall confess that wherein he hath sinned;

6. And he shall bring his forfeit unto the LORD for his sin which he hath sinned, a female from the flock, a lamb or a goat, for a sin-offering; and the priest shall make atonement for him as concerning his sin.

7. And if his means suffice not for a lamb, then he shall bring his forfeit for that wherein he hath sinned, two turtle-doves, or two young pigeons, unto the LORD: one for a sin-offering, and the other for a burnt-offering.

8. And he shall bring them unto the priest, who shall offer that which is for the sin-offering first, and pinch off its head close by its neck, but shall not divide it asunder.

9. And he shall sprinkle of the blood of the sin-offering upon the side of the altar; and the rest of the blood shall be drained out at the base of the altar; it is a sin-offering.

10. And he shall prepare the second for a burnt-offering, according to the ordinance; and the priest shall make atonement for him as concerning his sin which he hath sinned, and he shall be forgiven.

11. But if his means suffice not for two turtledoves, or two young pigeons, then he shall bring his offering for that wherein he hath sinned, the tenth part of an ephah of fine flour for a sin-offering; he shall put no oil upon it, neither shall he put any frankincense thereon; for it is a sin-offering.

12. And he shall bring it to the priest, and the priest shall take his handful of it as the memorial-part thereof, and make it smoke on the altar, upon the offerings of the LORD made by fire; it is a sin-offering.

13. And the priest shall make atonement for him as touching his sin that he hath sinned in any of these things, and he shall be forgiven; and the remnant shall be the priests, as the meal-offering.

14. And the LORD spoke unto Moses, saying:

15. If any one commit a trespass, and sin through error, in the holy things of the LORD, then he shall bring his forfeit unto the LORD, a ram without blemish out of the flock, according to thy valuation in silver by shekels, after the shekel of the sanctuary, for a guilt-offering.

16. And he shall make restitution for that which he hath done amiss in the holy thing, and shall add the fifth part thereto, and give it unto the priest; and the priest shall make atonement for him with the ram of the guilt-offering, and he shall be forgiven.

17. And if any one sin, and do any of the things which the LORD hath commanded not to be done, though he know it not, yet is he guilty, and shall bear his iniquity.

18. And he shall bring a ram without blemish out of the flock, according to thy valuation, for a guilt-offering, unto the priest; and the priest shall make atonement for him concerning the error which he committed, though he knew it not, and he shall be forgiven.

19. It is a guilt-offering-he is certainly guilty before the LORD.

20. And the LORD spoke unto Moses, saying:

21. If any one sin, and commit a trespass against the LORD, and deal falsely with his neighbour in a matter of deposit, or of pledge, or of robbery, or have oppressed his neighbour;

22. Or have found that which was lost, and deal falsely therein, and swear to a lie; in any of all these that a man doeth, sinning therein;

23. Then it shall be, if he hath sinned, and is guilty, that he shall restore that which he took by robbery, or the thing which he hath gotten by oppression, or the deposit which was deposited with him, or the lost thing which he found,

24. Or any thing about which he hath sworn falsely, he shall even restore it in full, and shall add the fifth part more thereto; unto him to whom it appertaineth shall he give it, in the day of his being guilty.

25. And he shall bring his forfeit unto the LORD, a ram without blemish out of the flock, according to thy valuation, for a guilt-offering, unto the priest.

26. And the priest shall make atonement for him before the LORD, and he shall be forgiven, concerning whatsoever he doeth so as to be guilty thereby.

Tzav

Chapter 6

1. And the LORD spoke unto Moses, saying:

2. Command Aaron and his sons, saying: This is the law of the burnt-offering: it is that which goeth up on its firewood upon the altar all night unto the morning; and the fire of the altar shall be kept burning thereby.

3. And the priest shall put on his linen garment, and his linen breeches shall he put upon his flesh; and he shall take up the ashes whereto the fire hath consumed the burnt-offering on the altar, and he shall put them beside the altar.

4. And he shall put off his garments, and put on other garments, and carry forth the ashes without the camp unto a clean place.

5. And the fire upon the altar shall be kept burning thereby, it shall not go out; and the priest shall kindle wood on it every morning; and he shall lay the burnt-offering in order upon it, and shall make smoke thereon the fat of the peace-offerings.

6. Fire shall be kept burning upon the altar continually; it shall not go out.

7. And this is the law of the meal-offering: the sons of Aaron shall offer it before the LORD, in front of the altar.

8. And he shall take up therefrom his handful, of the fine flour of the meal-offering, and of the oil thereof, and all the frankincense which is upon the meal-offering, and shall make the memorial-part thereof smoke upon the altar for a sweet savour unto the LORD.

9. And that which is left thereof shall Aaron and his sons eat; it shall be eaten without leaven in a holy place; in the court of the tent of meeting they shall eat it.

10. It shall not be baked with leaven. I have given it as their portion of My offerings made by fire; it is most holy, as the sin-offering, and as the guilt-offering.

11. Every male among the children of Aaron may eat of it, as a due for ever throughout your generations, from the offerings of the LORD made by fire; whatsoever toucheth them shall be holy.

12. And the LORD spoke unto Moses, saying:

13. This is the offering of Aaron and of his sons, which they shall offer unto the LORD in the day when he is anointed: the tenth part of an ephah of fine flour for a meal-offering perpetually, half of it in the morning, and half thereof in the evening.

14. On a griddle it shall be made with oil; when it is soaked, thou shalt bring it in; in broken pieces shalt thou offer the meal-offering for a sweet savour unto the LORD.

15. And the anointed priest that shall be in his stead from among his sons shall offer it, it is a due for ever; it shall be wholly made to smoke unto the LORD.

16. And every meal-offering of the priest shall be wholly made to smoke; it shall not be eaten.

17. And the LORD spoke unto Moses, saying:

18. Speak unto Aaron and to his sons, saying: This is the law of the sin-offering: in the place where the burnt-offering is killed shall the sin-offering be killed before the LORD; it is most holy.

19. The priest that offereth it for sin shall eat it; in a holy place shall it be eaten, in the court of the tent of meeting.

20. Whatsoever shall touch the flesh thereof shall be holy; and when there is sprinkled of the blood thereof upon any garment, thou shalt wash that whereon it was sprinkled in a holy place.

21. But the earthen vessel wherein it is sodden shall be broken; and if it be sodden in a brazen vessel, it shall be scoured, and rinsed in water.

22. Every male among the priests may eat thereof; it is most holy.

23. And no sin-offering, whereof any of the blood is brought into the tent of meeting to make atonement in the holy place, shall be eaten; it shall be burnt with fire.

Chapter 7

1. And this is the law of the guilt-offering: it is most holy.

2. In the place where they kill the burnt-offering shall they kill the guilt-offering: and the blood thereof shall be dashed against the altar round about.

3. And he shall offer of it all the fat thereof: the fat tail, and the fat that covereth the inwards,

4. And the two kidneys, and the fat that is on them, which is by the loins, and the lobe above the liver, which he shall take away by the kidneys.

5. And the priest shall make them smoke upon the altar for an offering made by fire unto the LORD; it is a guilt-offering.

6. Every male among the priests may eat thereof; it shall be eaten in a holy place; it is most holy.

7. As is the sin-offering, so is the guilt-offering; there is one law for them; the priest that maketh atonement therewith, he shall have it.

8. And the priest that offereth any man's burnt-offering, even the priest shall have to himself the skin of the burnt-offering which he hath offered.

9. And every meal-offering that is baked in the oven, and all that is dressed in the stewing-pan, and on the griddle, shall be the priest's that offereth it.

10. And every meal-offering, mingled with oil, or dry, shall all the sons of Aaron have, one as well as another.

11. And this is the law of the sacrifice of peace-offerings, which one may offer unto the LORD.

12. If he offer it for a thanksgiving, then he shall offer with the sacrifice of thanksgiving unleavened cakes mingled with oil, and unleavened wafers spread with oil, and cakes mingled with oil, of fine flour soaked.

13. With cakes of leavened bread he shall present his offering with the sacrifice of his peace-offerings for thanksgiving.

14. And of it he shall present one out of each offering for a gift unto the LORD; it shall be the priest's that dasheth the blood of the peace-offerings against the altar.

15. And the flesh of the sacrifice of his peace-offerings for thanksgiving shall be eaten on the day of his offering; he shall not leave any of it until the morning.

16. But if the sacrifice of his offering be a vow, or a freewill-offering, it shall be eaten on the day that he offereth his sacrifice; and on the morrow that which remaineth of it may be eaten.

17. But that which remaineth of the flesh of the sacrifice on the third day shall be burnt with fire.

18. And if any of the flesh of the sacrifice of his peace-offerings be at all eaten on the third day, it shall not be accepted, neither shall it be imputed unto him that offereth it; it shall be an abhorred thing, and the soul that eateth of it shall bear his iniquity.

19. And the flesh that toucheth any unclean thing shall not be eaten; it shall be burnt with fire. And as for the flesh, every one that is clean may eat thereof.

20. But the soul that eateth of the flesh of the sacrifice of peace-offerings, that pertain unto the LORD, having his uncleanness upon him, that soul shall be cut off from his people.

21. And when any one shall touch any unclean thing, whether it be the uncleanness of man, or an unclean beast, or any unclean detestable thing, and eat of the flesh of the sacrifice of peace-offerings, which pertain unto the LORD, that soul shall be cut off from his people.

22. And the LORD spoke unto Moses, saying:

23. Speak unto the children of Israel, saying: Ye shall eat no fat, of ox, or sheep, or goat.

24. And the fat of that which dieth of itself, and the fat of that which is torn of beasts, may be used for any other service; but ye shall in no wise eat of it.

25. For whosoever eateth the fat of the beast, of which men present an offering made by fire unto the LORD, even the soul that eateth it shall be cut off from his people.

26. And ye shall eat no manner of blood, whether it be of fowl or of beast, in any of your dwellings.

27. Whosoever it be that eateth any blood, that soul shall be cut off from his people.

28. And the LORD spoke unto Moses, saying:

29. Speak unto the children of Israel, saying: He that

offereth his sacrifice of peace-offerings unto the LORD shall bring his offering unto the LORD out of his sacrifice of peace-offerings.

30. His own hands shall bring the offerings of the LORD made by fire: the fat with the breast shall he bring, that the breast may be waved for a wave-offering before the LORD.

31. And the priest shall make the fat smoke upon the altar; but the breast shall be Aaron's and his sons.

32. And the right thigh shall ye give unto the priest for a heave-offering out of your sacrifices of peace-offerings.

33. He among the sons of Aaron, that offereth the blood of the peace-offerings, and the fat, shall have the right thigh for a portion.

34. For the breast of waving and the thigh of heaving have I taken of the children of Israel out of their sacrifices of peace-offerings, and have given them unto Aaron the priest and unto his sons as a due for ever from the children of Israel.

35. This is the consecrated portion of Aaron, and the consecrated portion of his sons, out of the offerings of the LORD made by fire, in the day when they were presented to minister unto the LORD in the priest's office;

36. Which the LORD commanded to be given them of the children of Israel, in the day that they were anointed. It is a due for ever throughout their generations.

37. This is the law of the burnt-offering, of the meal-offering, and of the sin-offering, and of the guilt-offering, and of the consecration-offering, and of the sacrifice of peace-offerings;

38. Which the LORD commanded Moses in mount Sinai, in the day that he commanded the children of Israel to present their offerings unto the LORD, in the wilderness of Sinai.

Chapter 8

1. And the LORD spoke unto Moses, saying:

2. Take Aaron and his sons with him, and the garments, and the anointing oil, and the bullock of the sin-offering, and the two rams, and the basket of unleavened bread;

3. And assemble thou all the congregation at the door of the tent of meeting.

4. And Moses did as the LORD commanded him; and the congregation was assembled at the door of the tent of meeting.

5. And Moses said unto the congregation: This is the thing which the LORD hath commanded to be done.

6. And Moses brought Aaron and his sons, and washed them with water.

7. And he put upon him the tunic, and girded him with the girdle, and clothed him with the robe, and put the ephod upon him, and he girded him with the skilfully woven band of the ephod, and bound it unto him therewith.

8. And he placed the breastplate upon him; and in the breastplate he put the Urim and the Thummim.

9. And he set the mitre upon his head; and upon the mitre, in front, did he set the golden plate, the holy crown; as the LORD commanded Moses.

10. And Moses took the anointing oil, and anointed the tabernacle and all that was therein, and sanctified them.

11. And he sprinkled thereof upon the altar seven times, and anointed the altar and all its vessels, and the laver and its base, to sanctify them.

12. And he poured of the anointing oil upon Aaron's head, and anointed him, to sanctify him.

13. And Moses brought Aaron's sons, and clothed them with tunics, and girded them with girdles, and bound head-tires upon them; as the LORD commanded Moses.

14. And the bullock of the sin-offering was brought; and Aaron and his sons laid their hands upon the head of the bullock of the sin-offering.

15. And when it was slain, Moses took the blood, and put it upon the horns of the altar round about with his finger, and purified the altar, and poured out the remaining blood at the base of the altar, and sanctified it, to make atonement for it.

16. And he took all the fat that was upon the inwards, and the lobe of the liver, and the two kidneys, and their fat, and Moses made it smoke upon the altar.

17. But the bullock, and its skin, and its flesh, and its dung, were burnt with fire without the camp; as the LORD commanded Moses.

18. And the ram of the burnt-offering was presented; and Aaron and his sons laid their hands upon the head of the ram.

19. And when it was killed, Moses dashed the blood against the altar round about.

20. And when the ram was cut into its pieces, Moses made the head, and the pieces, and the suet smoke.

21. And when the inwards and the legs were washed with water, Moses made the whole ram smoke upon the altar; it was a burnt-offering for a sweet savour; it was an offering made by fire unto the LORD; as the LORD commanded Moses.

22. And the other ram was presented, the ram of consecration, and Aaron and his sons laid their hands upon the head of the ram.

23. And when it was slain, Moses took of the blood thereof, and put it upon the tip of Aaron's right ear, and upon the thumb of his right hand, and upon the great toe of his right foot.

24. And Aaron's sons were brought, and Moses put of the blood upon the tip of their right ear, and upon the thumb of their right hand, and upon the great toe of their right foot; and Moses dashed the blood against the altar round about.

25. And he took the fat, and the fat tail, and all the fat that was upon the inwards, and the lobe of the liver, and the two kidneys, and their fat, and the right thigh.

26. And out of the basket of unleavened bread, that was before the LORD, he took one unleavened cake, and one cake of oiled bread, and one wafer, and placed them on the fat, and upon the right thigh.

27. And he put the whole upon the hands of Aaron, and upon the hands of his sons, and waved them for a wave-offering before the LORD.

28. And Moses took them from off their hands, and made them smoke on the altar upon the burnt-offering; they were a consecration-offering for a sweet savour; it was an offering made by fire unto the LORD.

29. And Moses took the breast, and waved it for a wave offering before the LORD; it was Moses' portion of the ram of consecration; as the LORD commanded Moses.

30. And Moses took of the anointing oil, and of the blood which was upon the altar, and sprinkled it upon Aaron, and upon his garments, and upon his sons, and upon his sons' garments with him, and sanctified Aaron, and his garments, and his sons, and his sons' garments with him.

31. And Moses said unto Aaron and to his sons: Boil the flesh at the door of the tent of meeting; and there eat it and the bread that is in the basket of consecration, as I commanded, saying: Aaron and his sons shall eat it.

32. And that which remaineth of the flesh and of the bread shall ye burn with fire.

33. And ye shall not go out from the door of the tent of meeting seven days, until the days of your consecration be fulfilled; for He shall consecrate you seven days.

34. As hath been done this day, so the LORD hath commanded to do, to make atonement for you.

35. And at the door of the tent of meeting shall ye abide day and night seven days, and keep the charge of the LORD, that ye die not; for so I am commanded.

36. And Aaron and his sons did all the things which the LORD commanded by the hand of Moses.

Shmini

Chapter 9

1. And it came to pass on the eighth day, that Moses called Aaron and his sons, and the elders of Israel;

2. And he said unto Aaron: Take thee a bull-calf for a sin-offering, and a ram for a burnt-offering, without blemish, and offer them before the LORD.

3. And unto the children of Israel thou shalt speak, saying: Take ye a he-goat for a sin-offering; and a calf and a lamb, both of the first year, without blemish, for a burnt-offering;

4. And an ox and a ram for peace-offerings, to sacrifice before the LORD; and a meal-offering mingled with oil; for to-day the LORD appeareth unto you.

5. And they brought that which Moses commanded before the tent of meeting; and all the congregation drew near and stood before the LORD.

6. And Moses said: This is the thing which the LORD commanded that ye should do; that the glory of the LORD may appear unto you.

7. And Moses said unto Aaron: Draw near unto the altar, and offer thy sin-offering, and thy burnt-offering, and make atonement for thyself, and for the people; and present the offering of the people, and make atonement for them; as the LORD commanded.

8. So, Aaron drew near unto the altar, and slew the calf of the sin-offering, which was for himself.

9. And the sons of Aaron presented the blood unto him; and he dipped his finger in the blood, and put it upon the horns of the altar, and poured out the blood at the base of the altar.

10. But the fat, and the kidneys, and the lobe of the liver of the sin-offering, he made smoke upon the altar; as the LORD commanded Moses.

11. And the flesh and the skin were burnt with fire without the camp.

12. And he slew the burnt-offering; and Aaron's sons delivered unto him the blood, and he dashed it against the altar round about.

13. And they delivered the burnt-offering unto him, piece by piece, and the head; and he made them smoke upon the altar.

14. And he washed the inwards and the legs, and

made them smoke upon the burnt-offering on the altar.

15. And the people's offering was presented; and he took the goat of the sin-offering which was for the people, and slew it, and offered it for sin, as the first.

16. And the burnt-offering was presented; and he offered it according to the ordinance.

17. And the meal-offering was presented; and he filled his hand therefrom, and made it smoke upon the altar, besides the burnt-offering of the morning.

18. He slew also the ox and the ram, the sacrifice of peace-offerings, which was for the people; and Aaron's sons delivered unto him the blood, and he dashed it against the altar round about,

19. And the fat of the ox, and of the ram, the fat tail, and that which covereth the inwards, and the kidneys, and the lobe of the liver.

20. And they put the fat upon the breasts, and he made the fat smoke upon the altar.

21. And the breasts and the right thigh Aaron waved for a wave-offering before the LORD; as Moses commanded.

22. And Aaron lifted up his hands toward the people, and blessed them; and he came down from offering the sin-offering, and the burnt-offering, and the peace-offerings.

23. And Moses and Aaron went into the tent of meeting, and came out, and blessed the people; and the glory of the LORD appeared unto all the people.

24. And there came forth fire from before the LORD, and consumed upon the altar the burnt-offering and the fat; and when all the people saw it, they shouted, and fell on their faces.

Chapter 10

1. And Nadab and Abihu, the sons of Aaron, took each of them his censer, and put fire therein, and laid incense thereon, and offered strange fire before the LORD, which He had not commanded them.

2. And there came forth fire from before the LORD, and devoured them, and they died before the LORD.

3. Then Moses said unto Aaron: This is it that the LORD spoke, saying: Through them that are nigh unto Me I will be sanctified, and before all the people I will be glorified. And Aaron held his peace.

4. And Moses called Mishael and Elzaphan, the sons of Uzziel the uncle of Aaron, and said unto them: Draw near, carry your brethren from before the sanctuary out of the camp.

5. So, they drew near, and carried them in their tunics out of the camp, as Moses had said.

6. And Moses said unto Aaron, and unto Eleazar and unto Ithamar, his sons: Let not the hair of your heads go loose, neither rend your clothes, that ye die not, and that He be not wroth with all the congregation; but let your brethren, the whole house of Israel, bewail the burning which the LORD hath kindled.

7. And ye shall not go out from the door of the tent of

meeting, lest ye die; for the anointing oil of the LORD is upon you. And they did according to the word of Moses.

8. And the LORD spoke unto Aaron, saying:

9. Drink no wine nor strong drink, thou, nor thy sons with thee, when ye go into the tent of meeting, that ye die not; it shall be a statute forever throughout your generations.

10. And that ye may put difference between the holy and the common, and between the unclean and the clean;

11. And that ye may teach the children of Israel all the statutes which the LORD hath spoken unto them by the hand of Moses.

12. And Moses spoke unto Aaron, and unto Eleazar and unto Ithamar, his sons that were left: Take the meal-offering that remaineth of the offerings of the LORD made by fire, and eat it without leaven beside the altar; for it is most holy.

13. And ye shall eat it in a holy place, because it is thy due, and thy sons due, of the offerings of the LORD made by fire; for so I am commanded.

14. And the breast of waving and the thigh of heaving shall ye eat in a clean place; thou, and thy sons, and thy daughters with thee; for they are given as thy due, and thy sons due, out of the sacrifices of the peace-offerings of the children of Israel.

15. The thigh of heaving and the breast of waving shall they bring with the offerings of the fat made by fire, to wave it for a wave-offering before the LORD; and it shall be thine, and thy sons with thee, as a due for ever; as the LORD hath commanded.

16. And Moses diligently inquired for the goat of the sin-offering, and, behold, it was burnt; and he was angry with Eleazar and with Ithamar, the sons of Aaron that were left, saying:

17. Wherefore have ye not eaten the sin-offering in the place of the sanctuary, seeing it is most holy, and He hath given it you to bear the iniquity of the congregation, to make atonement for them before the LORD?

18. Behold, the blood of it was not brought into the sanctuary within; ye should certainly have eaten it in the sanctuary, as I commanded.

19. And Aaron spoke unto Moses: Behold, this day have they offered their sin-offering and their burnt-offering before the LORD, and there have befallen me such things as these; and if I had eaten the sin-offering to-day, would it have been well-pleasing in the sight of the LORD?

20. And when Moses heard that, it was well-pleasing in his sight.

Chapter 11

1. And the LORD spoke unto Moses and to Aaron, saying unto them:

2. Speak unto the children of Israel, saying: These are the living things which ye may eat among all the beasts that are on the earth.

3. Whatsoever parteth the hoof, and is wholly cloven-footed, and cheweth the cud, among the beasts, that may ye eat.

4. Nevertheless, these shall ye not eat of them that only chew the cud, or of them that only part the hoof: the camel, because he cheweth the cud but parteth not the hoof, he is unclean unto you.

5. And the rock-badger, because he cheweth the cud but parteth not the hoof, he is unclean unto you.

6. And the hare, because she cheweth the cud but parteth not the hoof, she is unclean unto you.

7. And the swine, because he parteth the hoof, and is cloven-footed, but cheweth not the cud, he is unclean unto you.

8. Of their flesh ye shall not eat, and their carcasses ye shall not touch; they are unclean unto you.

9. These may ye eat of all that are in the waters: whatsoever hath fins and scales in the waters, in the seas, and in the rivers, them may ye eat.

10. And all that have not fins and scales in the seas, and in the rivers, of all that swarm in the waters, and of all the living creatures that are in the waters, they are a detestable thing unto you,

11. And they shall be a detestable thing unto you; ye shall not eat of their flesh, and their carcasses ye shall have in detestation.

12. Whatsoever hath no fins nor scales in the waters, that is a detestable thing unto you.

13. And these ye shall have in detestation among the fowls; they shall not be eaten, they are a detestable thing: the great vulture, and the bearded vulture, and the ospray;

14. And the kite, and the falcon after its kinds;

15. Every raven after its kinds;

16. And the ostrich, and the night-hawk, and the sea-mew, and the hawk after its kinds;

17. And the little owl, and the cormorant, and the great owl;

18. And the horned owl, and the pelican, and the carrion-vulture;

19. And the stork, and the heron after its kinds, and the hoopoe, and the bat.

20. All winged swarming things that go upon all fours are a detestable thing unto you.

21. Yet these may ye eat of all winged swarming things that go upon all fours, which have jointed legs above their feet, wherewith to leap upon the earth;

22. Even these of them ye may eat: the locust after its kinds, and the bald locust after its kinds, and the cricket after its kinds, and the grasshopper after its kinds.

23. But all winged swarming things, which have four feet, are a detestable thing unto you.

24. And by these ye shall become unclean; whosoever toucheth the carcass of them shall be unclean until even.

25. And whosoever beareth aught of the carcass of

them shall wash his clothes, and be unclean until the even.

26. Every beast which parteth the hoof, but is not cloven footed, nor cheweth the cud, is unclean unto you; every one that to toucheth them shall be unclean.

27. And whatsoever goeth upon its paws, among all beasts that go on all fours, they are unclean unto you; whoso toucheth their carcass shall be unclean until the even.

28. And he that beareth the carcass of them shall wash his clothes, and be unclean until the even; they are unclean unto you.

29. And these are they which are unclean unto you among the swarming things that swarm upon the earth: the weasel, and the mouse, and the great lizard after its kinds,

30. And the gecko, and the land-crocodile, and the lizard, and the sand-lizard, and the chameleon.

31. These are they which are unclean to you among all that swarm; whosoever doth touch them, when they are dead, shall be unclean until the even.

32. And upon whatsoever any of them, when they are dead, doth fall, it shall be unclean; whether it be any vessel of wood, or raiment, or skin, or sack, whatsoever vessel it be, wherewith any work is done, it must be put into water, and it shall be unclean until the even; then shall it be clean.

33. And every earthen vessel whereinto any of them falleth, whatsoever is in it shall be unclean, and it ye shall break.

34. All food therein which may be eaten, that on which water cometh, shall be unclean; and all drink in every such vessel that may be drunk shall be unclean.

35. And every thing whereupon any part of their carcass falleth shall be unclean; whether oven, or range for pots, it shall be broken in pieces; they are unclean, and shall be unclean unto you.

36. Nevertheless, a fountain or a cistern wherein is a gathering of water shall be clean; but he who toucheth their carcass shall be unclean.

37. And if aught of their carcass fall upon any sowing seed which is to be sown, it is clean.

38. But if water be put upon the seed, and aught of their carcass fall thereon, it is unclean unto you.

39. And if any beast, of which ye may eat, die, he that toucheth the carcass thereof shall be unclean until the even.

40. And he that eateth of the carcass of it shall wash his clothes, and be unclean until the even; he also that beareth the carcass of it shall wash his clothes, and be unclean until the even.

41. And every swarming thing that swarmeth upon the earth is a detestable thing; it shall not be eaten.

42. Whatsoever goeth upon the belly, and whatsoever goeth upon all fours, or whatsoever hath many feet, even all swarming things that swarm upon the earth, them ye shall not eat; for they are a detestable thing.

43. Ye shall not make yourselves detestable with any swarming thing that swarmeth, neither shall ye make yourselves unclean with them, that ye should be defiled thereby.

44. For I am the LORD your God; sanctify yourselves therefore, and be ye holy; for I am holy; neither shall ye defile yourselves with any manner of swarming thing that moveth upon the earth.

45. For I am the LORD that brought you up out of the land of Egypt, to be your God; ye shall therefore be holy, for I am holy.

46. This is the law of the beast, and of the fowl, and of every living creature that moveth in the waters, and of every creature that swarmeth upon the earth;

47. To make a difference between the unclean and the clean, and between the living thing that may be eaten and the living thing that may not be eaten.

Tazria

Chapter 12

1. And the LORD spoke unto Moses, saying:

2. Speak unto the children of Israel, saying: If a woman be delivered, and bear a man-child, then she shall be unclean seven days; as in the days of the impurity of her sickness shall she be unclean.

3. And in the eighth day the flesh of his foreskin shall be circumcised.

4. And she shall continue in the blood of purification

three and thirty days; she shall touch no hallowed thing, nor come into the sanctuary, until the days of her purification be fulfilled.

5. But if she bear a maid-child, then she shall be unclean two weeks, as in her impurity; and she shall continue in the blood of purification threescore and six days.

6. And when the days of her purification are fulfilled, for a son, or for a daughter, she shall bring a lamb of the first year for a burnt-offering, and a young pigeon, or a turtle-dove, for a sin-offering, unto the door of the tent of meeting, unto the priest.

7. And he shall offer it before the LORD, and make atonement for her; and she shall be cleansed from the fountain of her blood. This is the law for her that beareth, whether a male or a female.

8. And if her means suffice not for a lamb, then she shall take two turtle-doves, or two young pigeons: the one for a burnt-offering, and the other for a sin-offering; and the priest shall make atonement for her, and she shall be clean.

Chapter 13

1. And the LORD spoke unto Moses and unto Aaron, saying:

2. When a man shall have in the skin of his flesh a rising, or a scab, or a bright spot, and it become in the skin of his flesh the plague of leprosy, then he shall be brought unto Aaron the priest, or unto one of his sons the priests.

3. And the priest shall look upon the plague in the skin of the flesh; and if the hair in the plague be turned white, and the appearance of the plague be deeper than the skin of his flesh, it is the plague of leprosy; and the priest shall look on him, and pronounce him unclean.

4. And if the bright spot be white in the skin of his flesh, and the appearance thereof be not deeper than the skin, and the hair thereof be not turned white, then the priest shall shut up him that hath the plague seven days.

5. And the priest shall look on him the seventh day; and, behold, if the plague stay in its appearance, and the plague be not spread in the skin, then the priest shall shut him up seven days more.

6. And the priest shall look on him again the seventh day; and, behold, if the plague be dim, and the plague be not spread in the skin, then the priest shall pronounce him clean: it is a scab; and he shall wash his clothes, and be clean.

7. But if the scab spread abroad in the skin, after that he hath shown himself to the priest for his cleansing, he shall show himself to the priest again.

8. And the priest shall look, and, behold, if the scab be spread in the skin, then the priest shall pronounce him unclean: it is leprosy.

9. When the plague of leprosy is in a man, then he shall be brought unto the priest.

10. And the priest shall look, and, behold, if there be a white rising in the skin, and it have turned the hair white, and there be quick raw flesh in the rising,

11. It is an old leprosy in the skin of his flesh, and the priest shall pronounce him unclean; he shall not shut him up; for he is unclean.

12. And if the leprosy break out abroad in the skin, and the leprosy cover all the skin of him that hath the plague from his head even to his feet, as far as appeareth to the priest;

13. Then the priest shall look; and, behold, if the leprosy have covered all his flesh, he shall pronounce him clean that hath the plague; it is all turned white: he is clean.

14. But whensoever raw flesh appeareth in him, he shall be unclean.

15. And the priest shall look on the raw flesh, and pronounce him unclean; the raw flesh is unclean: it is leprosy.

16. But if the raw flesh again be turned into white, then he shall come unto the priest;

17. And the priest shall look on him; and, behold, if the plague be turned into white, then the priest shall pronounce him clean that hath the plague: he is clean.

18. And when the flesh hath in the skin thereof a boil, and it is healed,

19. And in the place of the boil there is a white rising, or a bright spot, reddish-white, then it shall be shown to the priest.

20. And the priest shall look; and, behold, if the appearance thereof be lower than the skin, and the hair thereof be turned white, then the priest shall pronounce him unclean: it is the plague of leprosy, it hath broken out in the boil.

21. But if the priest look on it, and, behold, there be no white hairs therein, and it be not lower than the skin, but be dim, then the priest shall shut him up seven days.

22. And if it spread abroad in the skin, then the priest shall pronounce him unclean: it is a plague.

23. But if the bright spot stay in its place, and be not spread, it is the scar of the boil; and the priest shall pronounce him clean.

24. Or when the flesh hath in the skin thereof a burning by fire, and the quick flesh of the burning become a bright spot, reddish-white, or white;

25. Then the priest shall look upon it; and, behold, if the hair in the bright spot be turned white, and the appearance thereof be deeper than the skin, it is leprosy, it hath broken out in the burning; and the priest shall pronounce him unclean: it is the plague of leprosy.

26. But if the priest look on it, and, behold, there be no white hair in the bright spot, and it be no lower than the skin, but be dim; then the priest shall shut him up seven days.

27. And the priest shall look upon him the seventh day; if it spread abroad in the skin, then the priest shall pronounce him unclean: it is the plague of leprosy.

28. And if the bright spot stay in its place, and be not spread in the skin, but be dim, it is the rising of the burning, and the priest shall pronounce him clean; for it is the scar of the burning.

29. And when a man or woman hath a plague upon the head or upon the beard,

30. Then the priest shall look on the plague; and, behold, if the appearance thereof be deeper than the skin, and there be in it yellow thin hair, then the priest shall pronounce him unclean: it is a scall, it is leprosy of the head or of the beard.

31. And if the priest look on the plague of the scall, and, behold, the appearance thereof be not deeper than the skin, and there be no black hair in it, then the priest shall shut up him that hath the plague of the scall seven days.

32. And in the seventh day the priest shall look on the plague; and, behold, if the scall be not spread, and there be in it no yellow hair, and the appearance of the scall be not deeper than the skin,

33. Then he shall be shaven, but the scall shall he not shave; and the priest shall shut up him that hath the scall seven days more.

34. And in the seventh day the priest shall look on the scall; and, behold, if the scall be not spread in the skin, and the appearance thereof be not deeper than the skin, then the priest shall pronounce him clean;

and he shall wash his clothes, and be clean.

35. But if the scall spread abroad in the skin after his cleansing,

36. Then the priest shall look on him; and, behold, if the scall be spread in the skin, the priest shall not seek for the yellow hair: he is unclean.

37. But if the scall stay in its appearance, and black hair be grown up therein; the scall is healed, he is clean; and the priest shall pronounce him clean.

38. And if a man or a woman have in the skin of their flesh bright spots, even white bright spots;

39. Then the priest shall look; and, behold, if the bright spots in the skin of their flesh be of a dull white, it is a tetter, it hath broken out in the skin: he is clean.

40. And if a man's hair be fallen off his head, he is bald; yet is he clean.

41. And if his hair be fallen off from the front part of his head, he is forehead-bald; yet is he clean.

42. But if there be in the bald head, or the bald forehead, a reddish-white plague, it is leprosy breaking out in his bald head, or his bald forehead.

43. Then the priest shall look upon him; and, behold, if the rising of the plague be reddish-white in his bald head, or in his bald forehead, as the appearance of leprosy in the skin of the flesh,

44. He is a leprous man, he is unclean; the priest shall surely pronounce him unclean: his plague is in his head.

45. And the leper in whom the plague is, his clothes

shall be rent, and the hair of his head shall go loose, and he shall cover his upper lip, and shall cry: **Unclean, unclean.**

46. All the days wherein the plague is in him he shall be unclean; he is unclean; he shall dwell alone; without the camp shall his dwelling be.

47. And when the plague of leprosy is in a garment, whether it be a woolen garment, or a linen garment;

48. Or in the warp, or in the woof, whether they be of linen, or of wool; or in a skin, or in any thing made of skin.

49. If the plague be greenish or reddish in the garment, or in the skin, or in the warp, or in the woof, or in any thing of skin, it is the plague of leprosy, and shall be shown unto the priest.

50. And the priest shall look upon the plague, and shut up that which hath the plague seven days.

51. And he shall look on the plague on the seventh day: if the plague be spread in the garment, or in the warp, or in the woof, or in the skin, whatever service skin is used for, the plague is a malignant leprosy: it is unclean.

52. And he shall burn the garment, or the warp, or the woof, whether it be of wool or of linen, or any thing of skin, wherein the plague is; for it is a malignant leprosy; it shall be burnt in the fire.

53. And if the priest shall look, and, behold, the plague be not spread in the garment, or in the warp, or in the woof, or in any thing of skin;

54. Then the priest shall command that they wash the thing wherein the plague is, and he shall shut it up seven days more.

55. And the priest shall look, after that the plague is washed; and, behold, if the plague have not changed its colour, and the plague be not spread, it is unclean; thou shalt burn it in the fire; it is a fret, whether the bareness be within or without.

56. And if the priest look, and, behold, the plague be dim after the washing thereof, then he shall rend it out of the garment, or out of the skin, or out of the warp, or out of the woof.

57. And if it appear still in the garment, or in the warp, or in the woof, or in any thing of skin, it is breaking out, thou shalt burn that wherein the plague is with fire.

58. And the garment, or the warp, or the woof, or whatsoever thing of skin it be, which thou shalt wash, if the plague be departed from them, then it shall be washed the second time, and shall be clean.

59. This is the law of the plague of leprosy in a garment of wool or linen, or in the warp, or in the woof, or in any thing of skin, to pronounce it clean, or to pronounce it unclean.

Metzora

Chapter 14

1. And the LORD spoke unto Moses, saying:

2. This shall be the law of the leper in the day of his cleansing: he shall be brought unto the priest.

3. And the priest shall go forth out of the camp; and the priest shall look, and, behold, if the plague of leprosy be healed in the leper;

4. Then shall the priest command to take for him that is to be cleansed two living clean birds, and cedar-wood, and scarlet, and hyssop.

5. And the priest shall command to kill one of the birds in an earthen vessel over running water.

6. As for the living bird, he shall take it, and the cedar-wood, and the scarlet, and the hyssop, and shall dip them and the living bird in the blood of the bird that was killed over the running water.

7. And he shall sprinkle upon him that is to be cleansed from the leprosy seven times, and shall pronounce him clean, and shall let go the living bird into the open field.

8. And he that is to be cleansed shall wash his clothes, and shave off all his hair, and bathe himself in water, and he shall be clean; and after that he may come into the camp, but shall dwell outside his tent seven days.

9. And it shall be on the seventh day, that he shall shave all his hair off his head and his beard and his eyebrows, even all his hair he shall shave off; and he shall wash his clothes, and he shall bathe his flesh in water, and he shall be clean.

10. And on the eighth day he shall take two he-lambs without blemish, and one ewe-lamb of the first year without blemish, and three tenth parts of an ephah of fine flour for a meal-offering, mingled with oil, and one log of oil.

11. And the priest that cleanseth him shall set the man that is to be cleansed, and those things, before the LORD, at the door of the tent of meeting.

12. And the priest shall take one of the he-lambs, and offer him for a guilt-offering, and the log of oil, and wave them for a wave-offering before the LORD.

13. And he shall kill the he-lamb in the place where they kill the sin-offering and the burnt-offering, in the place of the sanctuary; for as the sin-offering is the priests, so is the guilt-offering; it is most holy.

14. And the priest shall take of the blood of the guilt-offering, and the priest shall put it upon the tip of the right ear of him that is to be cleansed, and upon the thumb of his right hand, and upon the great toe of his right foot.

15. And the priest shall take of the log of oil, and pour it into the palm of his own left hand.

16. And the priest shall dip his right finger in the oil that is in his left hand, and shall sprinkle of the oil with his finger seven times before the LORD.

17. And of the rest of the oil that is in his hand shall the priest put upon the tip of the right ear of him that is to be cleansed, and upon the thumb of his right hand, and upon the great toe of his right foot, upon the blood of the guilt-offering.

18. And the rest of the oil that is in the priest's hand he shall put upon the head of him that is to be cleansed; and the priest shall make atonement for him before the LORD.

19. And the priest shall offer the sin-offering, and make atonement for him that is to be cleansed because of his uncleanness; and afterward he shall kill the burnt-offering.

20. And the priest shall offer the burnt-offering and the meal-offering upon the altar; and the priest shall make atonement for him, and he shall be clean.

21. And if he be poor, and his means suffice not, then he shall take one he-lamb for a guilt-offering to be waved, to make atonement for him, and one tenth part of an ephah of fine flour mingled with oil for a meal-offering, and a log of oil;

22. And two turtle-doves, or two young pigeons, such as his means suffice for; and the one shall be a sin-offering, and the other a burnt-offering.

23. And on the eighth day he shall bring them for his cleansing unto the priest, unto the door of the tent of meeting, before the LORD.

24. And the priest shall take the lamb of the guilt-offering, and the log of oil, and the priest shall wave them for a wave-offering before the LORD.

25. And he shall kill the lamb of the guilt-offering, and the priest shall take of the blood of the guilt-offering, and put it upon the tip of the right ear of him that is to be cleansed, and upon the thumb of his right hand, and upon the great toe of his right foot.

26. And the priest shall pour of the oil into the palm of his own left hand.

27. And the priest shall sprinkle with his right finger some of the oil that is in his left hand seven times before the LORD.

28. And the priest shall put of the oil that is in his hand upon the tip of the right ear of him that is to be cleansed, and upon the thumb of his right hand, and upon the great toe of his right foot, upon the place of the blood of the guilt-offering.

29. And the rest of the oil that is in the priest's hand he shall put upon the head of him that is to be cleansed, to make atonement for him before the LORD.

30. And he shall offer one of the turtle-doves, or of the young pigeons, such as his means suffice for;

31. Even such as his means suffice for, the one for a sin-offering, and the other for a burnt-offering, with the meal-offering; and the priest shall make atonement for him that is to be cleansed before the LORD.

32. This is the law of him in whom is the plague of leprosy, whose means suffice not for that which pertaineth to his cleansing.

33. And the LORD spoke unto Moses and unto Aaron, saying:

34. When ye are come into the land of Canaan, which I give to you for a possession, and I put the plague of leprosy in a house of the land of your possession;

35. Then he that owneth the house shall come and tell the priest, saying: There seemeth to me to be as it were a plague in the house.

36. And the priest shall command that they empty the house, before the priest go in to see the plague, that all that is in the house be not made unclean; and afterward the priest shall go in to see the house.

37. And he shall look on the plague, and, behold, if the plague be in the walls of the house with hollow streaks, greenish or reddish, and the appearance thereof be lower than the wall;

38. Then the priest shall go out of the house to the door of the house, and shut up the house seven days.

39. And the priest shall come again the seventh day, and shall look; and, behold, if the plague be spread in the walls of the house;

40. Then the priest shall command that they take out the stones in which the plague is, and cast them into an unclean place without the city.

41. And he shall cause the house to be scraped within round about, and they shall pour out the mortar that they scrape off without the city into an unclean place.

42. And they shall take other stones, and put them in the place of those stones; and he shall take other mortar, and shall plaster the house.

43. And if the plague come again, and break out in the house, after that the stones have been taken out, and after the house hath been scraped, and after it is plastered;

44. Then the priest shall come in and look; and, behold, if the plague be spread in the house, it is a malignant leprosy in the house: it is unclean.

45. And he shall break down the house, the stones of it, and the timber thereof, and all the mortar of the house; and he shall carry them forth out of the city into an unclean place.

46. Moreover, he that goeth into the house all the while that it is shut up shall be unclean until the even.

47. And he that lieth in the house shall wash his clothes; and he that eateth in the house shall wash his clothes.

48. And if the priest shall come in, and look, and, behold, the plague hath not spread in the house, after the house was plastered; then the priest shall pronounce the house clean, because the plague is healed.

49. And he shall take to cleanse the house two birds, and cedar-wood, and scarlet, and hyssop.

50. And he shall kill one of the birds in an earthen vessel over running water.

51. And he shall take the cedar-wood, and the hyssop, and the scarlet, and the living bird, and dip them in the blood of the slain bird, and in the running water, and sprinkle the house seven times.

52. And he shall cleanse the house with the blood of the bird, and with the running water, and with the living bird, and with the cedar-wood, and with the hyssop, and with the scarlet.

53. But he shall let go the living bird out of the city into the open field; so, shall he make atonement for the house; and it shall be clean.

54. This is the law for all manner of plague of leprosy, and for a scall;

55. And for the leprosy of a garment, and for a house;

56. And for a rising, and for a scab, and for a bright spot;

57. To teach when it is unclean, and when it is clean; this is the law of leprosy.

Chapter 15

1. And the LORD spoke unto Moses and to Aaron, saying:

2. Speak unto the children of Israel, and say unto them: When any man hath an issue out of his flesh, his issue is unclean.

3. And this shall be his uncleanness in his issue: whether his flesh run with his issue, or his flesh be stopped from his issue, it is his uncleanness.

4. Every bed whereon he that hath the issue lieth shall be unclean; and every thing whereon he sitteth shall be unclean.

5. And whosoever toucheth his bed shall wash his clothes, and bathe himself in water, and be unclean until the even.

6. And he that sitteth on any thing whereon he that hath the issue sat shall wash his clothes, and bathe himself in water, and be unclean until the even.

7. And he that toucheth the flesh of him that hath the issue shall wash his clothes, and bathe himself in water, and be unclean until the even.

8. And if he that hath the issue spit upon him that is clean, then he shall wash his clothes, and bathe himself in water, and be unclean until the even.

9. And what saddle soever he that hath the issue rideth upon shall be unclean.

10. And whosoever toucheth any thing that was under him shall be unclean until the even; and he that beareth those things shall wash his clothes, and bathe himself in water, and be unclean until the even.

11. And whomsoever he that hath the issue toucheth, without having rinsed his hands in water, he shall wash his clothes, and bathe himself in water, and be unclean until the even.

12. And the earthen vessel, which he that hath the issue toucheth, shall be broken; and every vessel of wood shall be rinsed in water.

13. And when he that hath an issue is cleansed of his issue, then he shall number to himself seven days for his cleansing, and wash his clothes; and he shall bathe his flesh in running water, and shall be clean.

14. And on the eighth day he shall take to him two turtle-doves, or two young pigeons, and come before the LORD unto the door of the tent of meeting, and give them unto the priest.

15. And the priest shall offer them, the one for a sin-offering, and the other for a burnt-offering; and the priest shall make atonement for him before the LORD for his issue.

16. And if the flow of seed go out from a man, then he shall bathe all his flesh in water, and be unclean until the even.

17. And every garment, and every skin, whereon is the flow of seed, shall be washed with water, and be unclean until the even.

18. The woman also with whom a man shall lie carnally, they shall both bathe themselves in water, and be unclean until the even.

19. And if a woman have an issue, and her issue in her flesh be blood, she shall be in her impurity seven days; and whosoever toucheth her shall be unclean until the even.

20. And every thing that she lieth upon in her impurity shall be unclean; every thing also that she sitteth upon shall be unclean.

21. And whosoever toucheth her bed shall wash his clothes, and bathe himself in water, and be unclean until the even.

22. And whosoever toucheth any thing that she sitteth upon shall wash his clothes, and bathe himself in water, and be unclean until the even.

23. And if he be on the bed, or on any thing whereon she sitteth, when he toucheth it, he shall be unclean until the even.

24. And if any man lie with her, and her impurity be upon him, he shall be unclean seven days; and every bed whereon he lieth shall be unclean.

25. And if a woman have an issue of her blood many days not in the time of her impurity, or if she have an issue beyond the time of her impurity; all the days of the issue of her uncleanness she shall be as in the days of her impurity: she is unclean.

26. Every bed whereon she lieth all the days of her issue shall be unto her as the bed of her impurity; and every thing whereon she sitteth shall be unclean, as the uncleanness of her impurity.

27. And whosoever toucheth those things shall be unclean, and shall wash his clothes, and bathe himself in water, and be unclean until the even.

28. But if she be cleansed of her issue, then she shall number to herself seven days, and after that she shall be clean.

29. And on the eighth day she shall take unto her two turtle-doves, or two young pigeons, and bring them unto the priest, to the door of the tent of meeting.

30. And the priest shall offer the one for a sin-offering, and the other for a burnt-offering; and the priest shall make atonement for her before the LORD for the issue of her uncleanness.

31. Thus, shall ye separate the children of Israel from their uncleanness; that they die not in their uncleanness, when they defile My tabernacle that is in the midst of them.

32. This is the law of him that hath an issue, and of him from whom the flow of seed goeth out, so that he is unclean thereby;

33. And of her that is sick with her impurity, and of them that have an issue, whether it be a man, or a woman; and of him that lieth with her that is unclean.

Achrei Mot

Chapter 16

1. And the LORD spoke unto Moses, after the death of the two sons of Aaron, when they drew near before the LORD, and died;

2. And the LORD said unto Moses: Speak unto Aaron thy brother, that he come not at all times into the holy place within the veil, before the ark-cover which is upon the ark; that he die not; for I appear in the cloud upon the ark-cover.

3. Herewith shall Aaron come into the holy place: with a young bullock for a sin-offering, and a ram for a burnt-offering.

4. He shall put on the holy linen tunic, and he shall have the linen breeches upon his flesh, and shall be girded with the linen girdle, and with the linen mitre shall he be attired; they are the holy garments; and he shall bathe his flesh in water, and put them on.

5. And he shall take of the congregation of the children of Israel two he-goats for a sin-offering, and one ram for a burnt-offering.

6. And Aaron shall present the bullock of the sin-offering, which is for himself, and make atonement for himself, and for his house.

7. And he shall take the two goats, and set them before the LORD at the door of the tent of meeting.

8. And Aaron shall cast lots upon the two goats: one lot for the LORD, and the other lot for Azazel.

9. And Aaron shall present the goat upon which the lot fell for the LORD, and offer him for a sin-offering.

10. But the goat, on which the lot fell for Azazel, shall be set alive before the LORD, to make atonement over him, to send him away for Azazel into the wilderness.

11. And Aaron shall present the bullock of the sin-offering, which is for himself, and shall make atonement for himself, and for his house, and shall kill the bullock of the sin-offering which is for himself.

12. And he shall take a censer full of coals of fire from off the altar before the LORD, and his hands full of sweet incense beaten small, and bring it within the veil.

13. And he shall put the incense upon the fire before the LORD, that the cloud of the incense may cover the ark-cover that is upon the testimony, that he die not.

14. And he shall take of the blood of the bullock, and sprinkle it with his finger upon the ark-cover on the east; and before the ark-cover shall he sprinkle of the blood with his finger seven times.

15. Then shall he kill the goat of the sin-offering, that is for the people, and bring his blood within the veil, and do with his blood as he did with the blood of the bullock, and sprinkle it upon the ark-cover, and before the ark-cover.

16. And he shall make atonement for the holy place, because of the uncleannesses of the children of Israel, and because of their transgressions, even all their sins; and so, shall he do for the tent of meeting, that dwelleth with them in the midst of their uncleannesses.

17. And there shall be no man in the tent of meeting when he goeth in to make atonement in the holy place, until he come out, and have made atonement for himself, and for his household, and for all the assembly of Israel.

18. And he shall go out unto the altar that is before the LORD, and make atonement for it; and shall take of the blood of the bullock, and of the blood of the goat, and put it upon the horns of the altar round about.

19. And he shall sprinkle of the blood upon it with his finger seven times, and cleanse it, and hallow it from the uncleannesses of the children of Israel.

20. And when he hath made an end of atoning for the holy place, and the tent of meeting, and the altar, he shall present the live goat.

21. And Aaron shall lay both his hands upon the head of the live goat, and confess over him all the iniquities of the children of Israel, and all their transgressions, even all their sins; and he shall put them upon the head of the goat, and shall send him away by the hand of an appointed man into the wilderness.

22. And the goat shall bear upon him all their iniquities unto a land which is cut off; and he shall let go the goat in the wilderness.

23. And Aaron shall come into the tent of meeting, and shall put off the linen garments, which he put on when he went into the holy place, and shall leave them there.

24. And he shall bathe his flesh in water in a holy place and put on his other vestments, and come forth, and offer his burnt-offering and the burnt-offering of the people, and make atonement for himself and for the people.

25. And the fat of the sin-offering shall he make smoke upon the altar.

26. And he that letteth go the goat for Azazel shall wash his clothes, and bathe his flesh in water, and afterward he may come into the camp.

27. And the bullock of the sin-offering, and the goat of the sin-offering, whose blood was brought in to make atonement in the holy place, shall be carried forth without the camp; and they shall burn in the fire their skins, and their flesh, and their dung.

28. And he that burneth them shall wash his clothes, and bathe his flesh in water, and afterward he may come into the camp.

29. And it shall be a statute for ever unto you: in the

seventh month, on the tenth day of the month, ye shall afflict your souls, and shall do no manner of work, the home-born, or the stranger that sojourneth among you.

30. For on this day shall atonement be made for you, to cleanse you; from all your sins shall ye be clean before the LORD.

31. It is a sabbath of solemn rest unto you, and ye shall afflict your souls; it is a statute for ever.

32. And the priest, who shall be anointed and who shall be consecrated to be priest in his father's stead, shall make the atonement, and shall put on the linen garments, even the holy garments.

33. And he shall make atonement for the most holy place, and he shall make atonement for the tent of meeting and for the altar; and he shall make atonement for the priests and for all the people of the assembly.

34. And this shall be an everlasting statute unto you, to make atonement for the children of Israel because of all their sins once in the year. And he did as the LORD commanded Moses.

Chapter 17

1. And the LORD spoke unto Moses, saying:

2. Speak unto Aaron, and unto his sons, and unto all the children of Israel, and say unto them: This is the thing which the LORD hath commanded, saying:

3. What man soever there be of the house of Israel,

that killeth an ox, or lamb, or goat, in the camp, or that killeth it without the camp,

4. And hath not brought it unto the door of the tent of meeting, to present it as an offering unto the LORD before the tabernacle of the LORD, blood shall be imputed unto that man; he hath shed blood; and that man shall be cut off from among his people.

5. To the end that the children of Israel may bring their sacrifices, which they sacrifice in the open field, even that they may bring them unto the LORD, unto the door of the tent of meeting, unto the priest, and sacrifice them for sacrifices of peace-offerings unto the LORD.

6. And the priest shall dash the blood against the altar of the LORD at the door of the tent of meeting, and make the fat smoke for a sweet savour unto the LORD.

7. And they shall no more sacrifice their sacrifices unto the satyrs, after whom they go astray. This shall be a statute for ever unto them throughout their generations.

8. And thou shalt say unto them: Whatsoever man there be of the house of Israel, or of the strangers that sojourn among them, that offereth a burnt-offering or sacrifice,

9. And bringeth it not unto the door of the tent of meeting, to sacrifice it unto the LORD, even that man shall be cut off from his people.

10. And whatsoever man there be of the house of

Israel, or of the strangers that sojourn among them, that eateth any manner of blood, I will set My face against that soul that eateth blood, and will cut him off from among his people.

11. For the life of the flesh is in the blood; and I have given it to you upon the altar to make atonement for your souls; for it is the blood that maketh atonement by reason of the life.

12. Therefore, I said unto the children of Israel: No soul of you shall eat blood, neither shall any stranger that sojourneth among you eat blood.

13. And whatsoever man there be of the children of Israel, or of the strangers that sojourn among them, that taketh in hunting any beast or fowl that may be eaten, he shall pour out the blood thereof, and cover it with dust.

14. For as to the life of all flesh, the blood thereof is all one with the life thereof; therefore, I said unto the children of Israel: Ye shall eat the blood of no manner of flesh; for the life of all flesh is the blood thereof; whosoever eateth it shall be cut off.

15. And every soul that eateth that which dieth of itself, or that which is torn of beasts, whether he be home-born or a stranger, he shall wash his clothes, and bathe himself in water, and be unclean until the even; then shall he be clean.

16. But if he wash them not, nor bathe his flesh, then he shall bear his iniquity.

Chapter 18

1. And the LORD spoke unto Moses, saying:
Speak unto the children of Israel, and say unto them:
2. I am the LORD your God.
3. After the doings of the land of Egypt, wherein ye dwelt, shall ye not do; and after the doings of the land of Canaan, whither I bring you, shall ye not do; neither shall ye walk in their statutes.
4. Mine ordinances shall ye do, and My statutes shall ye keep, to walk therein: I am the LORD your God.
5. Ye shall therefore keep My statutes, and Mine ordinances, which if a man do, he shall live by them: I am the LORD.
6. None of you shall approach to any that is near of kin to him, to uncover their nakedness. I am the LORD.
7. The nakedness of thy father, and the nakedness of thy mother, shalt thou not uncover: she is thy mother; thou shalt not uncover her nakedness.
8. The nakedness of thy father's wife shalt thou not uncover: it is thy father's nakedness.
9. The nakedness of thy sister, the daughter of thy father, or the daughter of thy mother, whether born at home, or born abroad, even their nakedness thou shalt not uncover.
10. The nakedness of thy son's daughter, or of thy daughter's daughter, even their nakedness thou shalt not uncover; for theirs is thine own nakedness.
11. The nakedness of thy father's wife's daughter,

begotten of thy father, she is thy sister, thou shalt not uncover her nakedness.

12. Thou shalt not uncover the nakedness of thy father's sister: she is thy fathers near kinswoman.

13. Thou shalt not uncover the nakedness of thy mother's sister; for she is thy mothers near kinswoman.

14. Thou shalt not uncover the nakedness of thy father's brother, thou shalt not approach to his wife: she is thine aunt.

15. Thou shalt not uncover the nakedness of thy daughter-in-law: she is thy son's wife; thou shalt not uncover her nakedness.

16. Thou shalt not uncover the nakedness of thy brother's wife: it is thy brother's nakedness.

17. Thou shalt not uncover the nakedness of a woman and her daughter; thou shalt not take her son's daughter, or her daughter's daughter, to uncover her nakedness: they are near kinswomen; it is lewdness.

18. And thou shalt not take a woman to her sister, to be a rival to her, to uncover her nakedness, beside the other in her lifetime.

19. And thou shalt not approach unto a woman to uncover her nakedness, as long as she is impure by her uncleanness.

20. And thou shalt not lie carnally with thy neighbour's wife, to defile thyself with her.

21. And thou shalt not give any of thy seed to set them apart to Molech, neither shalt thou profane the name of thy God: I am the LORD.

22. Thou shalt not lie with mankind, as with womankind; it is abomination.

23. And thou shalt not lie with any beast to defile thyself therewith; neither shall any woman stand before a beast, to lie down thereto; it is perversion.

24. Defile not ye yourselves in any of these things; for in all these the nations are defiled, which I cast out from before you.

25. And the land was defiled, therefore I did visit the iniquity thereof upon it, and the land vomited out her inhabitants.

26. Ye therefore shall keep My statutes and Mine ordinances, and shall not do any of these abominations; neither the home-born, nor the stranger that sojourneth among you.

27. For all these abominations have the men of the land done, that were before you, and the land is defiled.

28. That the land vomit not you out also, when ye defile it, as it vomited out the nation that was before you.

29. For whosoever shall do any of these abominations, even the souls that do them shall be cut off from among their people.

30. Therefore, shall ye keep My charge, that ye do not any of these abominable customs, which were done before you, and that ye defile not yourselves therein: I am the LORD your God.

Kedoshim

Chapter 19

1. And the LORD spoke unto Moses, saying:

2. Speak unto all the congregation of the children of Israel, and say unto them: Ye shall be holy; for I the LORD your God am holy.

3. Ye shall fear every man his mother, and his father, and ye shall keep My sabbaths: I am the LORD your God.

4. Turn ye not unto the idols, nor make to yourselves molten gods: I am the LORD your God.

5. And when ye offer a sacrifice of peace-offerings unto the LORD, ye shall offer it that ye may be accepted.

6. It shall be eaten the same day ye offer it, and on the morrow; and if aught remain until the third day, it shall be burnt with fire.

7. And if it be eaten at all on the third day, it is a vile thing; it shall not be accepted.

8. But every one that eateth it shall bear his iniquity, because he hath profaned the holy thing of the LORD; and that soul shall be cut off from his people.

9. And when ye reap the harvest of your land, thou shalt not wholly reap the corner of thy field, neither shalt thou gather the gleaning of thy harvest.

10. And thou shalt not glean thy vineyard, neither shalt thou gather the fallen fruit of thy vineyard; thou shalt leave them for the poor and for the stranger: I am the LORD your God.

11. Ye shall not steal; neither shall ye deal falsely, nor lie one to another.

12. And ye shall not swear by My name falsely, so that thou profane the name of thy God: I am the LORD.

13. Thou shalt not oppress thy neighbour, nor rob him; the wages of a hired servant shall not abide with thee all night until the morning.

14. Thou shalt not curse the deaf, nor put a stumbling-block before the blind, but thou shalt fear thy God: I am the LORD.

15. Ye shall do no unrighteousness in judgment; thou shalt not respect the person of the poor, nor favour the person of the mighty; but in righteousness shalt thou judge thy neighbour.

16. Thou shalt not go up and down as a talebearer among thy people; neither shalt thou stand idly by the blood of thy neighbour: I am the LORD.

17. Thou shalt not hate thy brother in thy heart; thou shalt surely rebuke thy neighbour, and not bear sin because of him.

18. Thou shalt not take vengeance, nor bear any grudge against the children of thy people, but thou shalt love thy neighbour as thyself: I am the LORD.

19. Ye shall keep My statutes. Thou shalt not let thy cattle gender with a diverse kind; thou shalt not sow thy field with two kinds of seed; neither shall there come upon thee a garment of two kinds of stuff mingled together.

20. And whosoever lieth carnally with a woman, that is a bondmaid, designated for a man, and not at all redeemed, nor was freedom given her; there shall be inquisition; they shall not be put to death, because she was not free.

21. And he shall bring his forfeit unto the LORD, unto the door of the tent of meeting, even a ram for a guilt-offering.

22. And the priest shall make atonement for him with the ram of the guilt-offering before the LORD for his sin which he hath sinned; and he shall be forgiven for his sin which he hath sinned.

23. And when ye shall come into the land, and shall have planted all manner of trees for food, then ye shall count the fruit thereof as forbidden; three years shall it be as forbidden unto you; it shall not be eaten.

24. And in the fourth year all the fruit thereof shall be holy, for giving praise unto the LORD.

25. But in the fifth year may ye eat of the fruit thereof, that it may yield unto you more richly the increase thereof: I am the LORD your God.

26. Ye shall not eat with the blood; neither shall ye practise divination nor soothsaying.

27. Ye shall not round the corners of your heads, neither shalt thou mar the corners of thy beard.

28. Ye shall not make any cuttings in your flesh for the dead, nor imprint any marks upon you: I am the

LORD.

29. Profane not thy daughter, to make her a harlot, lest the land fall into harlotry, and the land become full of lewdness.

30. Ye shall keep My sabbaths, and reverence My sanctuary: I am the LORD.

31. Turn ye not unto the ghosts, nor unto familiar spirits; seek them not out, to be defiled by them: I am the LORD your God.

32. Thou shalt rise up before the hoary head, and honour the face of the old man, and thou shalt fear thy God: I am the LORD.

33. And if a stranger sojourn with thee in your land, ye shall not do him wrong.

34. The stranger that sojourneth with you shall be unto you as the home-born among you, and thou shalt love him as thyself; for ye were strangers in the land of Egypt: I am the LORD your God.

35. Ye shall do no unrighteousness in judgment, in meteyard, in weight, or in measure.

36. Just balances, just weights, a just ephah, and a just hin, shall ye have: I am the LORD your God, who brought you out of the land of Egypt.

37. And ye shall observe all My statutes, and all Mine ordinances, and do them: I am the LORD.

Chapter 20

1. And the LORD spoke unto Moses, saying:

2. Moreover, thou shalt say to the children of Israel:

Whosoever he be of the children of Israel, or of the strangers that sojourn in Israel, that giveth of his seed unto Molech; he shall surely be put to death; the people of the land shall stone him with stones.

3. I also will set My face against that man, and will cut him off from among his people, because he hath given of his seed unto Molech, to defile My sanctuary, and to profane My holy name.

4. And if the people of the land do at all hide their eyes from that man, when he giveth of his seed unto Molech, and put him not to death;

5. Then I will set My face against that man, and against his family, and will cut him off, and all that go astray after him, to go astray after Molech, from among their people.

6. And the soul that turneth unto the ghosts, and unto the familiar spirits, to go astray after them, I will even set My face against that soul, and will cut him off from among his people.

7. Sanctify yourselves therefore, and be ye holy; for I am the LORD your God.

8. And keep ye My statutes, and do them: I am the LORD who sanctify you.

9. For whatsoever man there be that curseth his father or his mother shall surely be put to death; he hath cursed his father or his mother; his blood shall be upon him.

10. And the man that committeth adultery with another man's wife, even he that committeth adultery with his neighbour's wife, both the adulterer and the adulteress shall surely be put to death.

11. And the man that lieth with his father's wife-he hath uncovered his father's nakedness-both of them shall surely be put to death; their blood shall be upon them.

12. And if a man lie with his daughter-in-law, both of them shall surely be put to death; they have wrought corruption; their blood shall be upon them.

13. And if a man lie with mankind, as with womankind, both of them have committed abomination: they shall surely be put to death; their blood shall be upon them.

14. And if a man take with his wife also her mother, it is wickedness: they shall be burnt with fire, both he and they; that there be no wickedness among you.

15. And if a man lie with a beast, he shall surely be put to death; and ye shall slay the beast.

16. And if a woman approach unto any beast, and lie down thereto, thou shalt kill the woman, and the beast: they shall surely be put to death; their blood shall be upon them.

17. And if a man shall take his sister, his father's daughter, or his mother's daughter, and see her nakedness, and she see his nakedness: it is a shameful thing; and they shall be cut off in the sight of the children of their people: he hath uncovered his sister's nakedness; he shall bear his iniquity.

18. And if a man shall lie with a woman having her

sickness, and shall uncover her nakedness-he hath made naked her fountain, and she hath uncovered the fountain of her blood-both of them shall be cut off from among their people.

19. And thou shalt not uncover the nakedness of thy mother's sister, nor of thy father's sister; for he hath made naked his near kin; they shall bear their iniquity.

20. And if a man shall lie with his uncle's wife-he hath uncovered his uncle's nakedness-they shall bear their sin; they shall die childless.

21. And if a man shall take his brother's wife, it is impurity: he hath uncovered his brother's nakedness; they shall be childless.

22. Ye shall therefore keep all My statutes, and all Mine ordinances, and do them, that the land, whither I bring you to dwell therein, vomit you not out.

23. And ye shall not walk in the customs of the nation, which I am casting out before you; for they did all these things, and therefore I abhorred them.

24. But I have said unto you: Ye shall inherit their land, and I will give it unto you to possess it, a land flowing with milk and honey. I am the LORD your God, who have set you apart from the peoples.

25. Ye shall therefore separate between the clean beast and the unclean, and between the unclean fowl and the clean; and ye shall not make your souls detestable by beast, or by fowl, or by any thing wherewith the ground teemeth, which I have set apart for you to hold unclean.

26. And ye shall be holy unto Me; for I the LORD am holy, and have set you apart from the peoples, that ye should be Mine.

27. A man also or a woman that divineth by a ghost or a familiar spirit, shall surely be put to death; they shall stone them with stones; their blood shall be upon them.

Emor

Chapter 21

1. And the LORD said unto Moses: Speak unto the priests the sons of Aaron, and say unto them: There shall none defile himself for the dead among his people;

2. Except for his kin, that is near unto him, for his mother, and for his father, and for his son, and for his daughter, and for his brother;

3. And for his sister a virgin, that is near unto him, that hath had no husband, for her may he defile himself.

4. He shall not defile himself, being a chief man among his people, to profane himself.

5. They shall not make baldness upon their head, neither shall they shave off the corners of their beard, nor make any cuttings in their flesh.

6. They shall be holy unto their God, and not profane the name of their God; for the offerings of the LORD made by fire, the bread of their God, they do offer;

therefore, they shall be holy.

7. They shall not take a woman that is a harlot, or profaned; neither shall they take a woman put away from her husband; for he is holy unto his God.

8. Thou shalt sanctify him therefore; for he offereth the bread of thy God; he shall be holy unto thee; for I the LORD, who sanctify you, am holy.

9. And the daughter of any priest, if she profane herself by playing the harlot, she profaneth her father: she shall be burnt with fire.

10. And the priest that is highest among his brethren, upon whose head the anointing oil is poured, and that is consecrated to put on the garments, shall not let the hair of his head go loose, nor rend his clothes;

11. Neither shall he go in to any dead body, nor defile himself for his father, or for his mother;

12. Neither shall he go out of the sanctuary, nor profane the sanctuary of his God; for the consecration of the anointing oil of his God is upon him: I am the LORD.

13. And he shall take a wife in her virginity.

14. A widow, or one divorced, or a profaned woman, or a harlot, these shall he not take; but a virgin of his own people shall he take to wife.

15. And he shall not profane his seed among his people; for I am the LORD who sanctify him.

16. And the LORD spoke unto Moses, saying:

17. Speak unto Aaron, saying: Whosoever he be of thy seed throughout their generations that hath a blemish, let him not approach to offer the bread of his God.

18. For whatsoever man he be that hath a blemish, he shall not approach: a blind man, or a lame, or he that hath any thing maimed, or anything too long,

19. Or a man that is broken-footed, or broken-handed,

20. Or crook-backed, or a dwarf, or that hath his eye overspread, or is scabbed, or scurvy, or hath his stones crushed;

21. No man of the seed of Aaron the priest, that hath a blemish, shall come nigh to offer the offerings of the LORD made by fire; he hath a blemish; he shall not come nigh to offer the bread of his God.

22. He may eat the bread of his God, both of the most holy, and of the holy.

23. Only he shall not go in unto the veil, nor come nigh unto the altar, because he hath a blemish; that he profane not My holy places; for I am the LORD who sanctify them.

24. So, Moses spoke unto Aaron, and to his sons, and unto all the children of Israel.

Chapter 22

1. And the LORD spoke unto Moses, saying:

2. Speak unto Aaron and to his sons, that they separate themselves from the holy things of the children of Israel, which they hallow unto Me, and that they profane not My holy name: I am the LORD.

3. Say unto them: Whosoever he be of all your seed

throughout your generations, that approacheth unto the holy things, which the children of Israel hallow unto the LORD, having his uncleanness upon him, that soul shall be cut off from before Me: I am the LORD.

4. What man soever of the seed of Aaron is a leper, or hath an issue, he shall not eat of the holy things, until he be clean. And whoso toucheth any one that is unclean by the dead; or from whomsoever the flow of seed goeth out;

5. Or whosoever toucheth any swarming thing, whereby he may be made unclean, or a man of whom he may take uncleanness, whatsoever uncleanness he hath;

6. The soul that toucheth any such shall be unclean until the even, and shall not eat of the holy things, unless he bathe his flesh in water.

7. And when the sun is down, he shall be clean; and afterward he may eat of the holy things, because it is his bread.

8. That which dieth of itself, or is torn of beasts, he shall not eat to defile himself therewith: I am the LORD.

9. They shall therefore keep My charge, lest they bear sin for it, and die therein, if they profane it: I am the LORD who sanctify them.

10. There shall no common man eat of the holy thing; a tenant of a priest, or a hired servant, shall not eat of the holy thing.

11. But if a priest buy any soul, the purchase of his money, he may eat of it; and such as are born in his house, they may eat of his bread.

12. And if a priest's daughter be married unto a common man, she shall not eat of that which is set apart from the holy things.

13. But if a priest's daughter be a widow, or divorced, and have no child, and is returned unto her father's house, as in her youth, she may eat of her father's bread; but there shall no common man eat thereof.

14. And if a man eat of the holy thing through error, then he shall put the fifth part thereof unto it, and shall give unto the priest the holy thing.

15. And they shall not profane the holy things of the children of Israel, which they set apart unto the LORD;

16. And so, cause them to bear the iniquity that bringeth guilt, when they eat their holy things; for I am the LORD who sanctify them.

17. And the LORD spoke unto Moses, saying:

18. Speak unto Aaron, and to his sons, and unto all the children of Israel, and say unto them: Whosoever he be of the house of Israel, or of the strangers in Israel, that bringeth his offering, whether it be any of their vows, or any of their free-will-offerings, which are brought unto the LORD for a burnt-offering;

19. That ye may be accepted, ye shall offer a male without blemish, of the beeves, of the sheep, or of the goats.

20. But whatsoever hath a blemish, that shall ye not bring; for it shall not be acceptable for you.

21. And whosoever bringeth a sacrifice of peace-offerings unto the LORD in fulfilment of a vow clearly uttered, or for a freewill-offering, of the herd or of the flock, it shall be perfect to be accepted; there shall be no blemish therein.

22. Blind, or broken, or maimed, or having a wen, or scabbed, or scurvy, ye shall not offer these unto the LORD, nor make an offering by fire of them upon the altar unto the LORD.

23. Either a bullock or a lamb that hath any thing too long or too short, that mayest thou offer for a freewill-offering; but for a vow it shall not be accepted.

24. That which hath its stones bruised, or crushed, or torn, or cut, ye shall not offer unto the LORD; neither shall ye do thus in your land.

25. Neither from the hand of a foreigner shall ye offer the bread of your God of any of these, because their corruption is in them, there is a blemish in them; they shall not be accepted for you.

26. And the LORD spoke unto Moses, saying:

27. When a bullock, or a sheep, or a goat, is brought forth, then it shall be seven days under the dam; but from the eighth day and thenceforth it may be accepted for an offering made by fire unto the LORD.

28. And whether it be cow or ewe, ye shall not kill it and its young both in one day.

29. And when ye sacrifice a sacrifice of thanksgiving

unto the LORD, ye shall sacrifice it that ye may be accepted.

30. On the same day it shall be eaten; ye shall leave none of it until the morning: I am the LORD.

31. And ye shall keep My commandments, and do them: I am the LORD.

32. And ye shall not profane My holy name; but I will be hallowed among the children of Israel: I am the LORD who hallow you,

33. That brought you out of the land of Egypt, to be your God: I am the LORD.

Chapter 23

1. And the LORD spoke unto Moses, saying:

2. Speak unto the children of Israel, and say unto them: The appointed seasons of the LORD, which ye shall proclaim to be holy convocations, even these are My appointed seasons.

3. Six days shall work be done; but on the seventh day is a sabbath of solemn rest, a holy convocation; ye shall do no manner of work; it is a sabbath unto the LORD in all your dwellings.

4. These are the appointed seasons of the LORD, even holy convocations, which ye shall proclaim in their appointed season.

5. In the first month, on the fourteenth day of the month at dusk, is the LORD'S passover.

6. And on the fifteenth day of the same month is the feast of unleavened bread unto the LORD; seven days ye shall eat unleavened bread.

7. In the first day ye shall have a holy convocation; ye shall do no manner of servile work.

8. And ye shall bring an offering made by fire unto the LORD seven days; in the seventh day is a holy convocation; ye shall do no manner of servile work.

9. And the LORD spoke unto Moses saying:

10. Speak unto the children of Israel, and say unto them: When ye are come into the land which I give unto you, and shall reap the harvest thereof, then ye shall bring the sheaf of the first-fruits of your harvest unto the priest.

11. And he shall wave the sheaf before the LORD, to be accepted for you; on the morrow after the sabbath the priest shall wave it.

12. And in the day when ye wave the sheaf, ye shall offer a he-lamb without blemish of the first year for a burnt-offering unto the LORD.

13. And the meal-offering thereof shall be two tenth parts of an ephah of fine flour mingled with oil, an offering made by fire unto the LORD for a sweet savour; and the drink-offering thereof shall be of wine, the fourth part of a hin.

14. And ye shall eat neither bread, nor parched corn, nor fresh ears, until this selfsame day, until ye have brought the offering of your God; it is a statute for ever throughout your generations in all your dwellings.

15. And ye shall count unto you from the morrow

after the day of rest, from the day that ye brought the sheaf of the waving; seven weeks shall there be complete;

16. Even unto the morrow after the seventh week shall ye number fifty days; and ye shall present a new meal-offering unto the LORD.

17. Ye shall bring out of your dwellings two wave-loaves of two tenth parts of an ephah; they shall be of fine flour, they shall be baked with leaven, for first-fruits unto the LORD.

18. And ye shall present with the bread seven lambs without blemish of the first year, and one young bullock, and two rams; they shall be a burnt-offering unto the LORD, with their meal-offering, and their drink-offerings, even an offering made by fire, of a sweet savour unto the LORD.

19. And ye shall offer one he-goat for a sin-offering, and two he-lambs of the first year for a sacrifice of peace-offerings.

20. And the priest shall wave them with the bread of the first-fruits for a wave-offering before the LORD, with the two lambs; they shall be holy to the LORD for the priest.

21. And ye shall make proclamation on the selfsame day; there shall be a holy convocation unto you; ye shall do no manner of servile work; it is a statute for ever in all your dwellings throughout your generations.

22. And when ye reap the harvest of your land, thou

shalt not wholly reap the corner of thy field, neither shalt thou gather the gleaning of thy harvest; thou shalt leave them for the poor, and for the stranger: I am the LORD your God.

23. And the LORD spoke unto Moses, saying:

24. Speak unto the children of Israel, saying: In the seventh month, in the first day of the month, shall be a solemn rest unto you, a memorial proclaimed with the blast of horns, a holy convocation.

25. Ye shall do no manner of servile work; and ye shall bring an offering made by fire unto the LORD.

26. And the LORD spoke unto Moses, saying:

27. Howbeit on the tenth day of this seventh month is the day of atonement; there shall be a holy convocation unto you, and ye shall afflict your souls; and ye shall bring an offering made by fire unto the LORD.

28. And ye shall do no manner of work in that same day; for it is a day of atonement, to make atonement for you before the LORD your God.

29. For whatsoever soul it be that shall not be afflicted in that same day, he shall be cut off from his people.

30. And whatsoever soul it be that doeth any manner of work in that same day, that soul will I destroy from among his people.

31. Ye shall do no manner of work; it is a statute for ever throughout your generations in all your dwellings.

32. It shall be unto you a sabbath of solemn rest, and

ye shall afflict your souls; in the ninth day of the month at even, from even unto even, shall ye keep your sabbath.

33. And the LORD spoke unto Moses, saying:

34. Speak unto the children of Israel, saying: On the fifteenth day of this seventh month is the feast of tabernacles for seven days unto the LORD.

35. On the first day shall be a holy convocation; ye shall do no manner of servile work.

36. Seven days ye shall bring an offering made by fire unto the LORD; on the eighth day shall be a holy convocation unto you; and ye shall bring an offering made by fire unto the LORD; it is a day of solemn assembly; ye shall do no manner of servile work.

37. These are the appointed seasons of the LORD, which ye shall proclaim to be holy convocations, to bring an offering made by fire unto the LORD, a burnt-offering, and a meal-offering, a sacrifice, and drink-offerings, each on its own day;

38. Beside the sabbaths of the LORD, and beside your gifts, and beside all your vows, and beside all your freewill-offerings, which ye give unto the LORD.

39. Howbeit on the fifteenth day of the seventh month, when ye have gathered in the fruits of the land, ye shall keep the feast of the LORD seven days; on the first day shall be a solemn rest, and on the eighth day shall be a solemn rest.

40. And ye shall take you on the first day the fruit of goodly trees, branches of palm-trees, and boughs of thick trees, and willows of the brook, and ye shall rejoice before the LORD your God seven days.

41. And ye shall keep it a feast unto the LORD seven days in the year; it is a statute for ever in your generations; ye shall keep it in the seventh month.

42. Ye shall dwell in booths seven days; all that are home-born in Israel shall dwell in booths;

43. That your generations may know that I made the children of Israel to dwell in booths, when I brought them out of the land of Egypt: I am the LORD your God.

44. And Moses declared unto the children of Israel the appointed seasons of the LORD.

Chapter 24

1. And the LORD spoke unto Moses, saying:

2. Command the children of Israel, that they bring unto thee pure olive oil beaten for the light, to cause a lamp to burn continually.

3. Without the veil of the testimony, in the tent of meeting, shall Aaron order it from evening to morning before the LORD continually; it shall be a statute for ever throughout your generations.

4. He shall order the lamps upon the pure candlestick before the LORD continually.

5. And thou shalt take fine flour, and bake twelve cakes thereof: two tenth parts of an ephah shall be in one cake.

6. And thou shalt set them in two rows, six in a row,

upon the pure table before the LORD.

7. And thou shalt put pure frankincense with each row, that it may be to the bread for a memorial-part, even an offering made by fire unto the LORD.

8. Every sabbath day he shall set it in order before the LORD continually; it is from the children of Israel, an everlasting covenant.

9. And it shall be for Aaron and his sons; and they shall eat it in a holy place; for it is most holy unto him of the offerings of the LORD made by fire, a perpetual due.

10. And the son of an Israelitish woman, whose father was an Egyptian, went out among the children of Israel; and the son of the Israelitish woman and a man of Israel strove together in the camp.

11. And the son of the Israelitish woman blasphemed the Name, and cursed; and they brought him unto Moses. And his mother's name was Shelomith, the daughter of Dibri, of the tribe of Dan.

12. And they put him in ward, that it might be declared unto them at the mouth of the LORD.

13. And the LORD spoke unto Moses, saying:

14. Bring forth him that hath cursed without the camp; and let all that heard him lay their hands upon his head, and let all the congregation stone him.

15. And thou shalt speak unto the children of Israel, saying: Whosoever curseth his God shall bear his sin.

16. And he that blasphemeth the name of the LORD, he shall surely be put to death; all the congregation shall certainly stone him; as well the stranger, as the home-born, when he blasphemeth the Name, shall be put to death.

17. And he that smiteth any man mortally shall surely be put to death.

18. And he that smiteth a beast mortally shall make it good: life for life.

19. And if a man maim his neighbour; as he hath done, so shall it be done to him:

20. Breach for breach, eye for eye, tooth for tooth; as he hath maimed a man, so shall it be rendered unto him.

21. And he that killeth a beast shall make it good; and he that killeth a man shall be put to death.

22. Ye shall have one manner of law, as well for the stranger, as for the home-born; for I am the LORD your God.

23. And Moses spoke to the children of Israel, and they brought forth him that had cursed out of the camp, and stoned him with stones. And the children of Israel did as the LORD commanded Moses.

Behar

Chapter 25

1. And the LORD spoke unto Moses in mount Sinai, saying:

2. Speak unto the children of Israel, and say unto them: When ye come into the land which I give you,

then shall the land keep a sabbath unto the LORD.

3. Six years thou shalt sow thy field, and six years thou shalt prune thy vineyard, and gather in the produce thereof.

4. But in the seventh year shall be a sabbath of solemn rest for the land, a sabbath unto the LORD; thou shalt neither sow thy field, nor prune thy vineyard.

5. That which groweth of itself of thy harvest thou shalt not reap, and the grapes of thy undressed vine thou shalt not gather; it shall be a year of solemn rest for the land.

6. And the sabbath-produce of the land shall be for food for you: for thee, and for thy servant and for thy maid, and for thy hired servant and for the settler by thy side that sojourn with thee;

7. And for thy cattle, and for the beasts that are in thy land, shall all the increase thereof be for food.

8. And thou shalt number seven sabbaths of years unto thee, seven times seven years; and there shall be unto thee the days of seven sabbaths of years, even forty and nine years.

9. Then shalt thou make proclamation with the blast of the horn on the tenth day of the seventh month; in the day of atonement shall ye make proclamation with the horn throughout all your land.

10. And ye shall hallow the fiftieth year, and proclaim liberty throughout the land unto all the inhabitants thereof; it shall be a jubilee unto you; and ye shall return every man unto his possession, and ye shall return every man unto his family.

11. A jubilee shall that fiftieth year be unto you; ye shall not sow, neither reap that which groweth of itself in it, nor gather the grapes in it of the undressed vines.

12. For it is a jubilee; it shall be holy unto you; ye shall eat the increase thereof out of the field.

13. In this year of jubilee ye shall return every man unto his possession.

14. And if thou sell aught unto thy neighbour, or buy of thy neighbour's hand, ye shall not wrong one another.

15. According to the number of years after the jubilee thou shalt buy of thy neighbour, and according unto the number of years of the crops he shall sell unto thee.

16. According to the multitude of the years thou shalt increase the price thereof, and according to the fewness of the years thou shalt diminish the price of it; for the number of crops doth he sell unto thee.

17. And ye shall not wrong one another; but thou shalt fear thy God; for I am the LORD your God.

18. Wherefore ye shall do My statutes, and keep Mine ordinances and do them; and ye shall dwell in the land in safety.

19. And the land shall yield her fruit, and ye shall eat until ye have enough, and dwell therein in safety.

20. And if ye shall say: What shall we eat the seventh year? behold, we may not sow, nor gather in our increase;

21. Then I will command My blessing upon you in the sixth year, and it shall bring forth produce for the three years.

22. And ye shall sow the eighth year, and eat of the produce, the old store; until the ninth year, until her produce come in, ye shall eat the old store.

23. And the land shall not be sold in perpetuity; for the land is Mine; for ye are strangers and settlers with Me.

24. And in all the land of your possession ye shall grant a redemption for the land.

25. If thy brother be waxen poor, and sell some of his possession, then shall his kinsman that is next unto him come, and shall redeem that which his brother hath sold.

26. And if a man have no one to redeem it, and he be waxen rich and find sufficient means to redeem it;

27. Then let him count the years of the sale thereof, and restore the overplus unto the man to whom he sold it; and he shall return unto his possession.

28. But if he have not sufficient means to get it back for himself, then that which he hath sold shall remain in the hand of him that hath bought it until the year of jubilee; and in the jubilee it shall go out, and he shall return unto his possession.

29. And if a man sell a dwelling-house in a walled city, then he may redeem it within a whole year after it is sold; for a full year shall he have the right of redemption.

30. And if it be not redeemed within the space of a full year, then the house that is in the walled city shall be made sure in perpetuity to him that bought it, throughout his generations; it shall not go out in the jubilee.

31. But the houses of the villages which have no wall round about them shall be reckoned with the fields of the country; they may be redeemed, and they shall go out in the jubilee.

32. But as for the cities of the Levites, the houses of the cities of their possession, the Levites shall have a perpetual right of redemption.

33. And if a man purchase of the Levites, then the house that was sold in the city of his possession, shall go out in the jubilee; for the houses of the cities of the Levites are their possession among the children of Israel.

34. But the fields of the open land about their cities may not be sold; for that is their perpetual possession.

35. And if thy brother be waxen poor, and his means fail with thee; then thou shalt uphold him: as a stranger and a settler shall he live with thee.

36. Take thou no interest of him or increase; but fear thy God; that thy brother may live with thee.

37. Thou shalt not give him thy money upon interest, nor give him thy victuals for increase.

38. I am the LORD your God, who brought you forth out of the land of Egypt, to give you the land of

Canaan, to be your God.

39. And if thy brother be waxen poor with thee, and sell himself unto thee, thou shalt not make him to serve as a bondservant.

40. As a hired servant, and as a settler, he shall be with thee; he shall serve with thee unto the year of jubilee.

41. Then shall he go out from thee, he and his children with him, and shall return unto his own family, and unto the possession of his fathers shall he return.

42. For they are My servants, whom I brought forth out of the land of Egypt; they shall not be sold as bondmen.

43. Thou shalt not rule over him with rigour; but shalt fear thy God.

44. And as for thy bondmen, and thy bondmaids, whom thou mayest have: of the nations that are round about you, of them shall ye buy bondmen and bondmaids.

45. Moreover, of the children of the strangers that do sojourn among you, of them may ye buy, and of their families that are with you, which they have begotten in your land; and they may be your possession.

46. And ye may make them an inheritance for your children after you, to hold for a possession: of them may ye take your bondmen for ever; but over your brethren the children of Israel ye shall not rule, one over another, with rigour.

47. And if a stranger who is a settler with thee be

waxen rich, and thy brother be waxen poor beside him, and sell himself unto the stranger who is a settler with thee, or to the offshoot of a stranger's family,

48. After that he is sold he may be redeemed; one of his brethren may redeem him;

49. Or his uncle, or his uncle's son, may redeem him, or any that is nigh of kin unto him of his family may redeem him; or if he be waxen rich, he may redeem himself.

50. And he shall reckon with him that bought him from the year that he sold himself to him unto the year of jubilee; and the price of his sale shall be according unto the number of years; according to the time of a hired servant shall he be with him.

51. If there be yet many years, according unto them he shall give back the price of his redemption out of the money that he was bought for.

52. And if there remain but few years unto the year of jubilee, then he shall reckon with him; according unto his years shall he give back the price of his redemption.

53. As a servant hired year by year shall he be with him; he shall not rule with rigour over him in thy sight.

54. And if he be not redeemed by any of these means, then he shall go out in the year of jubilee, he, and his children with him.

55. For unto Me the children of Israel are servants; they are My servants whom I brought forth out of the land of Egypt: I am the LORD your God.

Chapter 26

1. Ye shall make you no idols, neither shall ye rear you up a graven image, or a pillar, neither shall ye place any figured stone in your land, to bow down unto it; for I am the LORD your God.

2. Ye shall keep My sabbaths, and reverence My sanctuary: I am the LORD.

Bechukotai

3. If ye walk in My statutes, and keep My commandments, and do them;

4. Then I will give your rains in their season, and the land shall yield her produce, and the trees of the field shall yield their fruit.

5. And your threshing shall reach unto the vintage, and the vintage shall reach unto the sowing time; and ye shall eat your bread until ye have enough, and dwell in your land safely.

6. And I will give peace in the land, and ye shall lie down, and none shall make you afraid; and I will cause evil beasts to cease out of the land, neither shall the sword go through your land.

7. And ye shall chase your enemies, and they shall fall before you by the sword.

8. And five of you shall chase a hundred, and a hundred of you shall chase ten thousand; and your enemies shall fall before you by the sword.

9. And I will have respect unto you, and make you fruitful, and multiply you; and will establish My covenant with you.

10. And ye shall eat old store long kept, and ye shall bring forth the old from before the new.

1. And I will set My tabernacle among you, and My soul shall not abhor you.

12. And I will walk among you, and will be your God, and ye shall be My people.

13. I am the LORD your God, who brought you forth out of the land of Egypt, that ye should not be their bondmen; and I have broken the bars of your yoke, and made you go upright.

14. But if ye will not hearken unto Me, and will not do all these commandments;

15. And if ye shall reject My statutes, and if your soul abhor Mine ordinances, so that ye will not do all My commandments, but break My covenant;

16. I also will do this unto you: I will appoint terror over you, even consumption and fever, that shall make the eyes to fail, and the soul to languish; and ye shall sow your seed in vain, for your enemies shall eat it.

17. And I will set My face against you, and ye shall be smitten before your enemies; they that hate you shall rule over you; and ye shall flee when none pursueth you.

18. And if ye will not yet for these things hearken

unto Me, then I will chastise you seven times more for your sins.

19. And I will break the pride of your power; and I will make your heaven as iron, and your earth as brass.

20. And your strength shall be spent in vain; for your land shall not yield her produce, neither shall the trees of the land yield their fruit.

21. And if ye walk contrary unto Me, and will not hearken unto Me; I will bring seven times more plagues upon you according to your sins.

22. And I will send the beast of the field among you, which shall rob you of your children, and destroy your cattle, and make you few in number; and your ways shall become desolate.

23. And if in spite of these things ye will not be corrected unto Me, but will walk contrary unto Me;

24. Then will I also walk contrary unto you; and I will smite you, even I, seven times for your sins.

25. And I will bring a sword upon you, that shall execute the vengeance of the covenant; and ye shall be gathered together within your cities; and I will send the pestilence among you; and ye shall be delivered into the hand of the enemy.

26. When I break your staff of bread, ten women shall bake your bread in one oven, and they shall deliver your bread again by weight; and ye shall eat, and not be satisfied.

27. And if ye will not for all this hearken unto Me,

but walk contrary unto Me;

28. Then I will walk contrary unto you in fury; and I also will chastise you seven times for your sins.

29. And ye shall eat the flesh of your sons, and the flesh of your daughters shall ye eat.

30. And I will destroy your high places, and cut down your sun-pillars, and cast your carcasses upon the carcasses of your idols; and My soul shall abhor you.

31. And I will make your cities a waste, and will bring your sanctuaries unto desolation, and I will not smell the savour of your sweet odours.

32. And I will bring the land into desolation; and your enemies that dwell therein shall be astonished at it.

33. And you will I scatter among the nations, and I will draw out the sword after you; and your land shall be a desolation, and your cities shall be a waste.

34. Then shall the land be paid her sabbaths, as long as it lieth desolate, and ye are in your enemies' land; even then shall the land rest, and repay her sabbaths.

35. As long as it lieth desolate it shall have rest; even the rest which it had not in your sabbaths, when ye dwelt upon it.

36. And as for them that are left of you, I will send a faintness into their heart in the lands of their enemies; and the sound of a driven leaf shall chase them; and they shall flee, as one fleeth from the sword; and they shall fall when none pursueth.

37. And they shall stumble one upon another, as it were before the sword, when none pursueth; and ye shall have no power to stand before your enemies.

38. And ye shall perish among the nations, and the land of your enemies shall eat you up.

39. And they that are left of you shall pine away in their iniquity in your enemies' lands; and also, in the iniquities of their fathers shall they pine away with them.

40. And they shall confess their iniquity, and the iniquity of their fathers, in their treachery which they committed against Me, and also that they have walked contrary unto Me.

41. I also will walk contrary unto them, and bring them into the land of their enemies; if then perchance their uncircumcised heart be humbled, and they then be paid the punishment of their iniquity;

42. Then will I remember My covenant with Jacob, and also My covenant with Isaac, and also My covenant with Abraham will I remember; and I will remember the land.

43. For the land shall lie forsaken without them, and shall be paid her sabbaths, while she lieth desolate without them; and they shall be paid the punishment of their iniquity; because, even because they rejected Mine ordinances, and their soul abhorred My statutes.

44. And yet for all that, when they are in the land of their enemies, I will not reject them, neither will I abhor them, to destroy them utterly, and to break My covenant with them; for I am the LORD their God.

45. But I will for their sakes remember the covenant

of their ancestors, whom I brought forth out of the land of Egypt in the sight of the nations, that I might be their God: I am the LORD.

46. These are the statutes and ordinances and laws, which the LORD made between Him and the children of Israel in mount Sinai by the hand of Moses.

Chapter 27

1. And the LORD spoke unto Moses, saying:

2. Speak unto the children of Israel, and say unto them: When a man shall clearly utter a vow of persons unto the LORD, according to thy valuation,

3. Then thy valuation shall be for the male from twenty years old even unto sixty years old, even thy valuation shall be fifty shekels of silver, after the shekel of the sanctuary.

4. And if it be a female, then thy valuation shall be thirty shekels.

5. And if it be from five years old even unto twenty years old, then thy valuation shall be for the male twenty shekels, and for the female ten shekels.

6. And if it be from a month old even unto five years old, then thy valuation shall be for the male five shekels of silver, and for the female thy valuation shall be three shekels of silver.

7. And if it be from sixty years old and upward: if it be a male, then thy valuation shall be fifteen shekels, and for the female ten shekels.

8. But if he be too poor for thy valuation, then he shall be set before the priest, and the priest shall value him; according to the means of him that vowed shall the priest value him.

9. And if it be a beast, whereof men bring an offering unto the LORD, all that any man giveth of such unto the LORD shall be holy.

10. He shall not alter it, nor change it, a good for a bad, or a bad for a good; and if he shall at all change beast for beast, then both it and that for which it is changed shall be holy.

11. And if it be any unclean beast, of which they may not bring an offering unto the LORD, then he shall set the beast before the priest.

12. And the priest shall value it, whether it be good or bad; as thou the priest valuest it, so shall it be.

13. But if he will indeed redeem it, then he shall add the fifth part thereof unto thy valuation.

14. And when a man shall sanctify his house to be holy unto the LORD, then the priest shall value it, whether it be good or bad; as the priest shall value it, so shall it stand.

15. And if he that sanctified it will redeem his house, then he shall add the fifth part of the money of thy valuation unto it, and it shall be his.

16. And if a man shall sanctify unto the LORD part of the field of his possession, then thy valuation shall be according to the sowing thereof; the sowing of a homer of barley shall be valued at fifty shekels of silver.

17. If he sanctify his field from the year of jubilee, according to thy valuation it shall stand.

18. But if he sanctify his field after the jubilee, then the priest shall reckon unto him the money according to the years that remain unto the year of jubilee, and an abatement shall be made from thy valuation.

19. And if he that sanctified the field will indeed redeem it, then he shall add the fifth part of the money of thy valuation unto it, and it shall be assured to him.

20. And if he will not redeem the field, or if he have sold the field to another man, it shall not be redeemed any more.

21. But the field, when it goeth out in the jubilee, shall be holy unto the LORD, as a field devoted; the possession thereof shall be the priests.

22. And if he sanctify unto the LORD a field which he hath bought, which is not of the field of his possession;

23. Then the priest shall reckon unto him the worth of thy valuation unto the year of jubilee; and he shall give thy valuation in that day, as a holy thing unto the LORD.

24. In the year of jubilee, the field shall return unto him of whom it was bought, even to him to whom the possession of the land belongeth.

25. And all thy valuations shall be according to the shekel of the sanctuary; twenty gerahs shall be the shekel.

26. Howbeit the firstling among beasts, which is born

as a firstling to the LORD, no man shall sanctify it; whether it be ox or sheep, it is the LORD'S.

27. And if it be of an unclean beast, then he shall ransom it according to thy valuation, and shall add unto it the fifth part thereof; or if it be not redeemed, then it shall be sold according to thy valuation.

28. Notwithstanding, no devoted thing, that a man may devote unto the LORD of all that he hath, whether of man or beast, or of the field of his possession, shall be sold or redeemed; every devoted thing is most holy unto the LORD.

29. None devoted, that may be devoted of men, shall be ransomed; he shall surely be put to death.

30. And all the tithe of the land, whether of the seed of the land, or of the fruit of the tree, is the LORD'S; it is holy unto the LORD.

31. And if a man will redeem aught of his tithe, he shall add unto it the fifth part thereof.

32. And all the tithe of the herd or the flock, whatsoever passeth under the rod, the tenth shall be holy unto the LORD.

33. He shall not inquire whether it be good or bad, neither shall he change it; and if he change it at all, then both it and that for which it is changed shall be holy; it shall not be redeemed.

34. These are the commandments, which the LORD commanded Moses for the children of Israel in mount Sinai.